A DARK FORCE

20 YEARS WITH A COVERT NARCISSIST

ERIN RILEY

DISCLAIMER:

Memories are subjective and imperfect, especially while living under stress. All of the events in this memoir are true to the best of the author's recollection. With respect to the privacy of others, some names, identifying characteristics, organizations, and locations have been changed.

Any thoughts, diagnoses, or opinions shared belong solely to the author and are not intended to malign any individual, organization, or company mentioned herein.

To Fabio for teaching me to love myself first.

THANK YOU:

Julian, you are braver than you believe…

Dar, my Sage

Paul Altobelli

Susan Drexler

Tom Moon

Lisa Seckler-Roode

Sally Stang

And Murphy, for sleeping in.

CONTENTS

1.
CHILDHOOD:
1959–1970

I was born in the era of *Mad Men*,[1] in fact, I <u>am</u> feisty little Sally Draper, only with dark brown hair. This was the age of *children should be seen and not heard; speak when spoken to; don't do as I do, do as I say; I'll give you something to cry about; that's none of your beeswax; because I said so, that's why; clean your plate, children are starving in Biafra;* and, *if you stick your tongue out it will stay that way.* Whenever I would ask my father "Hey Dad, where are we going?" he would quip, "Up Mikes!" which I soon learned to mean, it's none of your business (see beeswax above).

It seemed to me that my parents didn't care about my feelings; as a matter of fact, expressing feelings was not encouraged around my house. It was a bit Stepford-like[2] with everyone keeping to themselves and going about the business of each day. No hugs, no tender moments,

---

[1] *"Mad Men"* • An American period television drama series that aired from 2007 to 2015. Its fictional time period ran from 1960 to 1970.

[2] "Stepford-like" • A reference to the famous *Stepford Wives* novel about housewives in a small, idyllic Connecticut neighborhood who may actually be robots created by their husbands.

and very little eye contact. I remember my mom taking my picture as I cried saying, "This is to show you how ugly you look when you do that." I learned not to cry.

On the outside, we looked like the picture-perfect family. In 1969 we were featured in the *New York Times* article titled, "Housewives Who Slip Out of Aprons and Into Haute Couture,"[3] about high-fashion models who *had it all*, both a career and a family. On the inside, we were dead on arrival. My dad's lifelong battle with depression and alcoholism was swept under the rug and difficult and emotional discussions were avoided. Life went on day to day as *normal*, or at least what I knew to be normal.

I felt invisible to my parents but never took it personally. At the ripe old age of six, I thought it was kinda cool having complete freedom to come and go from our Upper West Side apartment at 90th & Broadway all by myself whenever I wanted to. It's not like anyone was looking for me, or looking out for me, for that matter. I walked to school by myself every day, and once a week I took the bus down Broadway, transferred to a second bus at the seediest stop of all, 42nd Street, and eventually down to Greenwich Village for dance classes after school. I could go to the store, Central Park, or a friend's house, come and go as I pleased with complete autonomy. I felt like a big girl in a big city, a grown-up lady… hey, what kid wouldn't want to make up their own rules? I was lucky, right? At least that's how I felt at the time, but internally

---

[3] Morris, Bernadine. "Housewives Who Slip Out of Aprons and Into Haute Couture." *The New York Times*, October 20, 1969, https://tinyurl.com/452xb4ps

my young brain was being hardwired for survival, independence, and self-reliance, living in a chronic state of hypervigilance and fight/flight.

Looking back on my childhood now, it's understandable that I didn't recognize my family as dysfunctional. It's not like I saw other kids' moms and dads slathering them with affection and praise while I was hanging out at their homes. I just figured kids had no rights and adults had all the power and that one day, when I finally turned 18, I would have rights too. Heck, they promised me I would, and of course, I believed them. They were my parents; why would they lie?

On my 18th birthday, I drove to the grocery store to exercise my newfound adult rights and bought my very first jar of Marshmallow Fluff to make "Fluffernutter"[4] sandwiches because my mom thought they were disgusting and refused to buy it for me. Ha, ha, MOM!

I never knew what was wrong with my family, but something felt *off*. I knew something was missing; I just couldn't put my finger on it. It was like we were four separate people, but not a family. I never once saw my parents kiss each other or hold hands. Dad rarely drank at home because Mom kept count, "Kevin, that's three." He did most of his drinking while away on business trips as a traveling salesman for Mary Quant and Yardley

---

[4] "Fluffernutter" • A peanut butter and marshmallow fluff sandwich.

Slicker.[5] It wasn't until I was 16 years old when I went into my dad's briefcase looking for makeup samples, but instead found several empty liquor bottles, and that's when I came to realize the extent of his addiction. *Why wouldn't he have put them in the trash? Hmm…*

This is when I learned my most valuable skill for trauma processing: cognitive dissonance.[6] I've learned that I can tell myself anything to make sense of a difficult situation, to help me survive. Unlearning this *talent* in my early 60s has turned out to be my life's biggest challenge, but my greatest reward.

Over the years, I sought the counsel of more therapists than I can count, but none of them were ever able to help me. I was led down the wrong path each time, thinking that as an emotionally-neglected child I MUST have low self-esteem, and therefore believe that I don't deserve to be loved, or that I somehow deserved to be mistreated and abandoned, but that was just not the case. I didn't know what love was, what it felt like, what to look for, or even who I really was inside.

When your parents don't reflect who you are back to you, your sense of self doesn't develop properly and you seek approval and validation from the

---

[5] "Mary Quant and Yardley Slicker" • Popular 1960s-era cosmetics companies.

[6] "Cognitive Dissonance" • Mental stress or discomfort experienced by an individual who holds two or more contradictory beliefs, ideas, or values at the same time.

outside, making you susceptible to predatory people until you can no longer deny your past. I believed that because I wasn't close with my dad growing up, I subliminally chose emotionally unavailable men, recreating that familiar scenario in my adult relationships but hoping to change the outcome. As it turned out, it was far more complex than that. I eventually came to learn that I was codependent and that Mom's stoicism and Dad's depression, coupled with my *Mad Men* upbringing, played a role in who I was to eventually become and the choices I was preprogrammed to make, again and again, and again.

When I was a little girl in New York City, I'd been fortunate to be able to make friends easily; my identity and self-worth developed through their love and acceptance of me. Whenever I would approach another child to ask them to play, they always said yes, so I figured I must be okay if the other kids want to be my friend. I made the softball team, I was a cheerleader, got invited to parties, and boys seemed to like me. I did well in school without even trying. I woke up every day in a good mood, and I still do. My mom called me Birdie because I was always the first in the family awake, belting show tunes in my room, much to the chagrin of the other family members. I became quite adept at hiding my negative or angry emotions and focusing only on the happy ones.

New York City was an epicenter of the civil rights movement in the early 1960s. In February 1964 (my kindergarten year at Rodeph Sholom[7]), the famed Freedom Day[8] was held to protest segregation in the New York City public school system. The citywide protest involved over half a million school children and teachers in an all-day walkout resulting in the institution of intercity busing throughout the five boroughs of New York. I was privileged to attend a terrific public school on the Upper West Side of Manhattan during this very special time in history, with a rainbow of friends of different cultures, family backgrounds, and socioeconomic classes. It gave me a great deal of empathy for others' life challenges throughout the rest of my life and influenced my intrinsic need to help those less fortunate. Being white, I knew I was lucky, and I felt guilty about it.

I believed I was naturally stronger than other people, that I could take more abuse and make do with less. I wasn't going to let it *bother me*. It was something I was proud of. We call this martyrdom; it runs deep in the fabric of my family going back many generations. It never occurred to me that I could choose more for myself; it was simply my lot in life, and life isn't fair, right? Everyone knows that. If I were ever involved in a multicar accident, I'd be the one doing triage. I never realized it was because I wasn't allowed to show weakness.

---

[7] "Rodeph Sholom" • An Independent Reform Jewish Day School in New York City.

[8] "Freedom Day" • The largest Civil Rights protest of the 1960s involving over 500,000 students, teachers, and supporters. Targeted was the New York City Public School System for failure to implement a reasonable integration plan, or repair the decaying infrastructure.

These are the internal messages in my brain. *You can handle it. Others have it worse than you. You are NOT a quitter.* When my dad passed out drunk at Mom's high school reunion, she told herself it was "not a reflection on her, but a reflection on him" and she wasn't going to let it *bother* her. I would often repeat those words to myself while living with an abuser.

When you have no tools in your toolbox, you are doomed to repeat your mistakes over and over again until you learn the hard way how to become your own best friend and prioritize yourself. I thought I was being a good person through self-sacrifice.

When I was about six years old, and my little brother was only four, Mom and Dad sat us down at the kitchen table to tell us they were getting a divorce and that we were moving with Mom to Boston to live with my aunt and uncle, grandparents, and six cousins, all under one roof. It is the one and only time I can remember being told what was happening before it actually happened. We boarded the bus at the Port Authority Bus Terminal and my aunt picked us up at South Station in Boston. Less than two weeks later, Grandma Helen sent us right back.

"Go home. You can't take care of two kids by yourself. So what if he drinks a little? Your dad was bedridden with multiple sclerosis. I never left him! You made your bed, you go lie in it" – a repeat performance of HER mom, my great-grandma, 'Little Gram's' words when Helen's 18-month-old son Andrew died of croup. "That's too bad, girl," was the only condolence she offered.

Little Gram had given birth to 13 children – two of them stillborn, two died in infancy, and the remaining nine traveled by boat from Newfoundland to Boston in April of 1929. At least she was left with nine healthy children and a brand-new start in the good old US of A! Unfortunately, it was just before the start of The Great Depression. *You're lucky to be here, take your lumps, and don't ever complain.* That's the generational attitude that's been passed down through the women in my family.

When I was born in 1959, women were often put under anesthesia for childbirth and my mom was no different. When she went into labor, my dad was out of town, as usual, pursuing his passion – acting in a theater production in New England. I'll explain more about this shortly. She hailed a cab to the hospital by herself, was immediately put to sleep, and 18 hours later I was removed by forceps and taken away to the nursery until the next day when I finally met some strange lady they told me was my mother. So, it's possible I may have experienced some VERY early abandonment trauma!

Mom told me I was bottle-fed because she couldn't make enough milk to satiate me but I always wondered if that was the entire story. *Did she need to work and have our housekeeper Adelaide feed me, or did she just feel uncomfortable being that close?* And what on earth motivated her to tell me that? *Erin, you're too much. Take it down a notch. You're too needy. You need too much attention. I can't even feed you!*

Infants look to their caregivers to learn how to regulate their emotions and process their surroundings. If the caregiver is emotionally unavailable or intermittently so, the child will grow up looking to external sources for attention and approval.

There was a 12-year difference between my parents, Kit and Kevin Riley. When they first met, Mom was only 22 and Dad almost 35, effortlessly charming, even dashing one might say. He was a tall, dark, ruggedly handsome New York City actor, with friends like Walter Matthau, Tony Curtis, and his closest friend, the Tony-nominated Nancy Marchand, best known for her role as Mrs. Pynchon on *Lou Grant* and the matriarch of *The Sopranos*, the acerbic Livia Soprano. My brother Chris and I grew up playing with Nancy's kids in the little courtyard nestled between our Upper West Side apartment buildings.

After her high school graduation, my mom began a modeling career in Boston and was swiftly discovered by an agent in New York City who relocated her to work in the Big Apple. She needed a place to stay so her new agent called my dad's agent (*how New York!*) knowing that my dad was engaged to a woman named Priscilla and often stayed at her apartment, leaving his own place unoccupied.

"Could a young model, Kitty Amory (a stage name given to her by her new agency), use your apartment for a month or two?"

"Of course!" said my dad.

So, young Kitty moved her 22-year-old self to NYC and enjoyed two peaceful weeks alone camping in my dad's apartment until one fateful night, when Dad drank too much and came home to the wrong apartment, and they met. I was born nine months later and Priscilla was suddenly single. They lied for years about their anniversary date as it was still *not okay* to have a child out of wedlock.

Mom did a lot to keep up with Kevin and his actor friends' drinking. There really was a *Mad Men* ethos at my home… neat drinks in tumblers, whiskey 'on the rocks' with glistening ice cubes, ashtrays full of cigarettes in various states of decay, men in business suits and ladies wearing tight shift dresses and gloves, their hairdos frozen solid. Mom played her role in that scene superbly but something had to give and that something was me.

During their parties, I was frequently placed in a playpen in the middle of the living room floor and one by one, the grownups would all fall asleep on the couches around me while I played with toys until I fell asleep too. No blanket, no goodnight kisses, no soft, comfortable crib; just a cold, hard playpen floor to sleep on. In the morning when the sun rose, I would wake up screaming from hunger and from cold, and my mom would crawl on her hands and knees across the living room floor to the kitchen, and return with a box of dry Cheerios and sprinkle them into the playpen over my head and go right back to bed.

I remember constantly trying to get her attention. She seemed so distant, so unattainable, icy-cold, and not one bit nurturing. I never felt like she could see me. She certainly couldn't hear me. She showed little emotion so I would call her SuperMom. Not because she was a super mom, but because she was stoic like the mannequin dress forms the fashion designers built their couture creations on. The wigs, the false eyelashes, the go-go boots, and micro-mini skirts were all the rage in the '60s; you just don't want your mom wearing them.

"I wish I were beautiful like you Mom."

"You'll just have to settle for pretty, Erin."

At least she wasn't lying to me this time. I would tap her on the arm repeatedly… *tap, tap, tap, tap, tap,* but she wouldn't even turn her head to look at me. If I really needed her, I might escalate my approach, and sometimes, but without looking my way, she would say, "I can't *heaaar* you when you whine," and walk away. I gave up trying. A precursor to both of my marriages, as you will soon come to learn.

When bullied on the playground, she told me, "the biggest shots are always the littlest shots." It helped me to develop empathy for bullies.

She wasn't all bad as a mom or directly cruel in any way. I do have many good memories, and at least she wasn't verbally shaming as she told me her mom was. She taught me how to do a cartwheel on the carpet, right in the middle of the living room of our apartment. We baked together – made donuts and hard candies. She took us to the Children's Zoo in Central Park and we rode the carousel. She even made snapdragons talk! I remember her showing me how to fold hospital corners while making the bed and how to push back my cuticles, but I really can't remember a whole lot more than that, and certainly no real-life lessons or guidance of any kind beyond the age of 10. She did make a few of our Halloween costumes, even though she rifled through our haul each year to grab all the candy corn and sesame candies. *Yuck, Mom, you can have them, along with those stale peeps you love so much and steal from my Easter basket every year.*

She was there in the house, things got done, but it felt like every man for himself in my family and that's how I learned to be so independent and to expect very little of others.

Family vacations were always to visit extended family in New England. Mom's relatives were just north of Boston, and my dad's parents lived on a private, expansive, 100-acre farm, at the end of a mile-long dirt driveway, overlooking Casco Bay, outside of Freeport, Maine. Most New Yorkers did not own an automobile, but because my dad traveled for work we were fortunate to have a wood-paneled station wagon that he parked on the street just outside our 90th Street apartment. My mom didn't learn to drive, not until she was 35.

Visiting my grandparents during the summer months was a welcome change from urban life. My brother and I picked wild blueberries on the farm and peeled layers of mica crystals off the rocks at the Atlantic shoreline. I started my sea glass collection there and added to it each time I visited the ocean for the next 50 years.

There were horseshoe crabs crawling all over the rocky beach and the air was fresh and clean. Being a city kid, it was an adventure to roam the property breathing in the crisp Maine air, discovering nature, and simply feeling free. I loved the ocean. It was so powerful, so majestic, and invigorating.

One summer we took a side trip to Cape Cod and rented a small saltbox house[9] balanced on the edge of a cliff, high above the water, with 100 rickety wooden steps leading down to a private beach. I remember sitting there with my legs hanging over that cliff and promising myself that I would work very hard my entire life if it meant I could one day live at the beach.

My parents never fought, but my brother and I sure made up for it. There's a funny family story from when I was very young, only 18 months old, and my mother asked me, "Would you like a little brother or sister to play with?" I thought about it for a minute and responded, "No, thanks," and went back to playing. I was certain of that; what little affection I got I wasn't going to share with some little brother! When they brought him home from the hospital I toddled into his room, took one look at him, and marched right back to my bedroom. I then collected all of my dolls and threw them one-by-one out

---

[9] "Saltbox House" • A triangular-roofed residential structure that is typically two stories high in front and one story in the rear.

of the bathroom window to their deaths below. *Pent-up frustration, Erin? Lack of parental attention?*

When I couldn't convince them to give him away, I shoved him off the bed and broke his collarbone. I never let him choose a TV show and if he tried to change the channel on me, I would punch him in the face and we would roll around on the floor wailing on each other. The signs of family dysfunction were all there but were never talked about. Point fingers at the symptoms but not the problems. One day I came home from school a few minutes early, just in time to catch my parents giving away my favorite cat Shadow, without so much as mentioning it to me in advance. How did they think I would feel about that? Oh right, feelings not allowed, especially negative ones.

I was 11 in 1970 when we left Manhattan for New Jersey. It was between 5th and 6th grade, perhaps the worst time in a young girl's life to take her away from her friends. Without friends or a strong family unit, I was adrift without sail or a rudder to guide me. As was most often the case, they neglected to let us know in advance we'd be moving. What rights do we have? None. We are children; our rights will come on our 18th birthday and not a moment sooner.

In 8th grade, when it came time for the birds and the bees talk, my mom walked into my bedroom and handed me a paperback book titled, *How a Baby is Made*, and without looking at me, mumbled, "Let me know if you have any questions… and I hope you don't," then walked right out. I had to learn everything on my own, or on the streets.

How did she get this way? One needs to look at the past to decipher the present and predict the future. She would refer to her mom as "The Shamer," although was never specific about why she would say that, but knowing Grandma Helen, it wasn't hard to imagine what messages were likely communicated to my mom when she was just a child. *"You're the pretty one, your sister is the smart one. We're going to send her to college and you're going to secretarial school."*

Instead of typing (a fate worse than death), she tried her hand at modeling and rose to the top of her field (ultimately working with such top-shelf designers as Norman Norell, Halston, and Yves Saint Laurent), but those inner-child wounds her mother inflicted stayed until she entered undergrad school at Rutgers University at the age of 42, eventually earning her Ph.D. in Psychology at 57.

Upon graduation, she opened her private practice in Flemington, NJ, and dedicated the rest of her life to helping others. She kept working until she was 77 because she had much to prove to her mom (*I am also smart!*), and also to herself. Not surprisingly, I followed the predictive protocol and would also feel the strong need to prove myself worthy of being seen and heard, and in the end, valued and loved by my mommy and daddy.

Her beloved and doting dad, George Pappas, worked as a foreman at General Electric until the age of 35 when he suddenly fell ill with multiple sclerosis. Over a period of several months, he began to stumble on his walk home and before long all the town was abuzz that he was a drunk. My mom was only seven years old when this happened, her older sister Gerry, barely 10. Things would never be the same after that and my mother was deeply affected by his illness.

The sisters were left alone to fend for themselves when Helen went to work at the local meat packing plant as a sausage stuffer. She needed to earn enough money for the family to eat when George could no longer support them financially. Martyrdom and self-sacrifice are deeply ingrained in the women in our family. *Count your blessings, don't complain.* Who knows how far back Transgenerational Epigenetic Inheritance[10] goes?

Back in those days, you did what you had to do to survive and there was no point in griping about it. George was for the most part bedridden from 35 until he died at the age of 66. The only exception was when he would transfer himself in his wheelchair to the adjoining room to use his Ham radio setup and talk to fascinating folks all around the world. He was a good man.

I forgave my mom for her shortcomings a long time ago.

---

[10] "Transgenerational Epigenetic Inheritance" • The theory of how behaviors and environment can cause changes that affect the way genes read a DNA sequence, i.e., a parent's experiences, in the form of epigenetic tags, can be passed down to future generations.

You cannot give what you did not receive. At the end of her life she became more like the mother I'd always wanted, giving me advice when I asked for it, telling me I was beautiful, and that she was proud of me.

My dad took a lot of beatings when he was a boy, both physical and emotional. He was the youngest of four children – three boys and a girl, Joanne, who was treated like one of the boys since she was very young. All the siblings were expected to work hard on the farm and in their studies. Grandpa was a snob and a proud graduate of Notre Dame University; he had high expectations of each of his offspring. For a few years, my dad and his brothers lived away from home, attending an exclusive private boarding school in Baltimore, because *nothing is too good for the Rileys.*

The genealogy of the Riley family has been thoroughly researched and is well-documented. It is said that the first English baby born in America on the Pilgrim ship, Mayflower, Peregrine White, was a direct ancestor of my father's mother, Genevieve White Riley. All the ladies in the Riley family are members of the DAR,[11] including yours truly.

Genevieve loved her four children with all her heart and did what she could to protect them from her husband's volatile temper, but over time, John Urban showed her

---

[11] "DAR" • The "Daughters of the American Revolution" is a lineage-based, nonprofit membership organization for women directly descended from an active participant in the United States' efforts toward independence in the 1770s.

and everyone else who ruled the roost. They did as he said, as he directed. It's where I can trace the emotional epigenetics of *children should be seen and not heard; speak when spoken to; don't do as I do, do as I say*, etc. My dad was her last hope to keep one of the babies at home, safely with her and helping in the kitchen. So young, curly blond Julian (later, "Kevin") got to hang out with his mom and learned to make a variety of meals for the family, a skill which served him well as a Merchant Marine cook on a ship in WWII, traveling around the world, preparing food for the other sailors.

His was an unhealthy environment to grow up in, which became far worse when the family's favorite brother Dick was killed in WWII. Everyone blamed everyone else. *How could Dick, the star son, be gone? Why wasn't it you? Or you? Or even YOU?* My uncle's death left my father with a deep depression that could only be managed with daily alcohol consumption, and what better place to hone your skills than on a WWII Merchant Marine boat out at sea with a bunch of other lonely men.

When he returned from the war his daily drinking continued, at first socially, until it became a true problem. He was a fun drunk and had plenty of bar buddies to hit the town with. In New York City, there's a bar on every corner and no one ever needs to drive themselves home. It was the '60s and alcohol was a very large and accepted part of daily culture.

2.

HIGH SCHOOL YEARS/ PARENTS' DIVORCE: 1970–1978

It was 1970 when my mom put her foot down, again.

"Kevin, if you don't quit drinking, I'm taking the kids and I'm leaving you, this time for real."

He knew she meant it and made her an offer she couldn't refuse. She knew if she left him, she really had nowhere else to go and her mother would only send her back home again; she had to hear him out and give him one final chance.

"What if we moved to the country? I could be like my dad, a distinguished country gentleman living on a farm. There would be less temptation, less stress; it would be easier to stay sober this time."

So, we moved to a sleepy little town outside of historic Lambertville, NJ, and purchased a 250-year-old fieldstone farmhouse on eight acres with a big barn and an outhouse for only $30,000. It had been a way station on the Underground Railroad[12] in pre–Civil War years, and came with lots of interesting history (but no indoor plumbing!). We spent the next eight years renovating it ourselves.

I was desperate to make friends at my new school but no one would give me the time of day. I'd never been shunned like that before. It was a horrible feeling. Being a child raised in a neglectful home meant I absolutely needed to have girlfriends, and I would do anything to be accepted by them. I became what's known as a people pleaser. If someone said to me, "Oh, I like your bracelet," I'd take it right off my arm and give it to them.

I thought if I exaggerated the truth just a little, the kids would think I was cooler than I was and maybe then they would like me; but it didn't work, and I became known as the class liar, a liar without any friends. Those were the days before social media and texting; I had lost touch with most of my elementary school friends from New York and was adrift in a sea of change, created by the adults who governed me.

Moving up to the high school in 7th grade didn't help much. Most of the Lambertville kids had been together since kindergarten, so I honed my people-pleasing skills and got craftier with the lies.

____

[12] "Underground Railroad" • A pre–Civil War network of people and places that helped escaped slaves find safe passage to the North. Most active from the 1790s to 1860s.

Without anyone to hang out with, I lost myself in the music of the 1970s. I felt the songwriters were my only friends. James Taylor's voice soothed me, and I would listen to his albums over and over and over again. *You've Got A Frie-e-end.* I discovered Joni Mitchell, who my mom loathed.

"Turn that shit off, Erin! She warbles like a bird, or are you just playing it at the wrong speed?"

Oh, shut up, Mom.

It was a great time for rock & roll, too. I would isolate myself upstairs in my bedroom, lying on the floor with my eyes closed, listening to bands like Aerosmith, Queen, Genesis, and Boston on my Bubble Dome Stereo System, complete with 8-track tape player, while holding the album jackets above my head, memorizing every single lyric as the music played on in my headphones. Once, I left the room for a few minutes and my mom snuck in to leave a vacuum there for me, hoping I might clean one day, but unaware that I had left Jethro Tull's "Bungle in the Jungle" on. When the song started with a loud lion's roar, she jumped right out of her skin and screamed. I laughed so hard.

I immersed myself in *Tommy,* by The Who, listening to it over and over again until I knew every word. I was completely mesmerized by the story and the amazing sounds that were emanating from my headphones and rippling through my entire body. It was the first double album I ever owned, and I'd saved up to purchase it with my own money from my job serving ice cream at Dilly's Corner. I felt a kinship with the main character, Tommy Walker, the Pinball Wizard. Tommy's mother had brainwashed him into believing that he did not see or hear his father murder his mother's lover, causing him to shut down all of his senses and retreat inward. In that moment, he became deaf, dumb, and blind to the outside world. My own mother spent most of her energy covering up my dad's drinking.

"Mom? Why is Dad sleeping on the living room floor?"

"Run along, honey. Nothing to see here."

"You didn't hear it, you didn't see it
You never heard it, not a word of it
You won't say nothing to no one
Never tell a soul, what you know is the truth"[13]

"See me, Feel me, Touch me, Heal me."

Tommy sang my pain for me.

It began when I was 14, sneaking alcohol from my parents' liquor cabinet. I would fill an empty mayonnaise jar with an ounce of vermouth, an ounce of gin, whiskey, vodka, and tequila. Then I'd replace what I took with water and bring the mayonnaise jar full of booze downtown to sit on the banks of the canal

---

[13] Townshend, Peter. "1921." "See Me Feel Me." *Tommy.* The Spirit Music Group. Hal Leonard. 1969.

with the other *bad girls* and drink it all down. One time, I blacked out and woke up the next day on the couch at my friend's house completely naked. I was scared and didn't know what had happened and of course, my parents were not concerned by my staying out all night, not one single bit. I could come and go as I pleased, just like when I was six in New York City.

Before I could drive, Mom would drop me off in the middle of downtown Lambertville to roam the streets with the other teens. On the nights she would come pick me up...

"You been smoking them funny cigarettes?"

No lecture, no scolding; she knew kids experimented because she used to climb out her bedroom window after her parents fell asleep and take the train to Boston to smoke cigarettes in jazz clubs. She never got caught.

While all this was going on, my parents were, as usual, preoccupied with their own lives and oblivious to my plight. There were no rules at my house and no one to teach us how to set proper boundaries or how to protect ourselves. As a boy, my brother Chris was fine with this but I was not, so I escalated my bad behavior in the hopes that someone, anyone, would come down on me and set a boundary. *Doesn't anyone care about Erin? Anyone?*

By the time I was a junior in high school, I was shoplifting daily from my job at JCPenney, skipping school, streaking through town (how very '70s!), spray painting graffiti on local area bridges, climbing the fence at the pool club to skinny-dip, driving drunk with open beer in the car… engaging in risky behaviors of all kinds. No one at home batted an eye.

While there were no outwardly visible signs of a dysfunctional family dynamic, we all fell into our respective roles: I was the family scapegoat, my brother the golden child. He was acting out too but like my mom, he never got caught. I wanted to get caught, desperately. I wanted them to put some rules down to protect us, but they never did. Chris loved not having a curfew; me, not so much.

My dad was drinking again, although I wasn't aware of it because he only drank while on business trips, but Mom was growing more resentful and the air in my home was as thick as pudding. I began picking fights with my dad, anything to get his attention, and at times it became quite scary; I thought he might hit me. If he was in one of his moods when my mom would need to leave the house, she would beg him not to hurt me while she was gone, yet she left me alone with him anyway.

This lack of parenting set me up to be abused by narcissistic men throughout my life. When you are looking for love anywhere you can find it, you can fall into some pretty-hard-to-get-out-of traps. I learned this the hardest way possible when in 1975 I attended a senior graduation party; I was only 15 years old, ripe to be taken advantage of, and the boys could smell it. Milling about the party I noticed the captain of the high school football team, Fes, staring right at me. I thought to myself, *if this guy likes me, I'm in!* He crossed the room and came over to speak to me.

"Hey, would you like to go for a ride in my car and drink a beer with me and Ty?"

Would I? I thought, grinning ear to ear inside. My nightmare was almost over… or had it just begun? I excitedly hopped into the back seat of his car with him and Ty in the front seat. He pulled around the corner, Ty got out and said, "Hey man, see you Monday at school," and Fes drove off. I wish I'd had parents to tell me to watch out for teenage boys. I had no idea that I was about to be raped in the front seat of a car on an abandoned highway outside of town. I didn't even know what was happening while it was happening, and worse yet, he fucking told everyone. When I came back to 11th grade the following September, 10 different guys asked me out the first week of school. For a girl who'd been formerly pretty unpopular, it was clear to me what had happened.

He was graduated and gone and I gained 70 pounds in under six months. Mom and Dad were concerned by my rapid weight gain; I'd always been a chubby kid but going from 134 pounds to 204 pounds that quickly was the first external sign of trouble within the family. They offered me money to lose weight, thinking somehow it must be their fault because Dad was drinking again. They had no idea that the real reason I needed to build a moat around me was for protection from boys, against rape. *If I could put a big fortress around me, they'll leave me alone.*

"Being fat weeds out assholes," declared my bestie April, who I met just a couple of years later while working at KROQ-FM in Los Angeles (the #1 Alt-Rock radio station in America). I didn't tell my mother I'd been raped for another 45 years, and when I finally did, the only condolence she offered was, "Oh, honey..." and then, "can you get me my scissors?"

Being fat does have its advantages. Teen boys, for the most part, left me alone for the last two years of school. I had to pay my ex-boyfriend Bobby to take me to the prom because no one wanted to take the fat girl, but he was sweet and I knew he truly cared about me from before I gained weight.

I continued on, pretending I was okay. Being bigger than the other girls, I was asked to be the bottom of the cheerleading pyramid holding up to seven other girls on my shoulders and bent knees. That only added to my internal narrative that I am stronger than others and can take more crap and somehow, that's a good thing.

Dad's drinking was obvious to us now and my acting out had escalated, so we entered family therapy at the Hunterdon County Medical Center in Flemington. During the very first session, the therapist looked at me and asked, "How does that make you feel?" and in true teenage spirit, I snarkily replied, "Where'd you get that one, page 99 of the shrink manual?" and stomped out right in the middle of the session, refusing to reenter the room.

The teachers at my school didn't know what to do with

me either. I would arrive at class after the bell rang, pass notes to the other students, and gossip during class. I was disrespectful and talked back to the teachers when they called me out for my disruptive behavior. Most of them sent me directly to the principal's office, cementing my self-belief that I was a bad kid and beyond help. I tested my French teacher like no other and to Lilie, I apologize!

There was one person in my life who seemed to know the right way to handle me, and I am forever grateful to Joanne Bunce, my high school music teacher. She couldn't fully replace the love I didn't receive at home, but she adopted a different approach from the other teachers, one that helped me to realize that if no one else was going to step up for me, I could step up for myself.

During band rehearsals, I would whisper to the kids next to me and miss cues so we'd all have to start over again from the top, calling attention to myself because… please, someone see that I'm in trouble. Whenever she would leave the room, I would put on a funk record and start a dance party, doing The Bump[14] with the boys until she would return, and then off to the principal's office I would march. She was at her wits' end and didn't know what to do with me; no one did.

But then, she concocted a brilliant idea, an idea that changed my life. Instead of punishing me, she gave me a solo, in Latin, a Vivaldi aria called "Qui sedes ad

---

[14] "The Bump" • A popular dance during the disco music years of the 1970s.

dexteram Patris" (Thou who sits at the right hand of the Father). I was to perform this solo in front of an audience of 200 parents, with a string quartet behind me and the entire 48-member chorus singing backup. She knew that if I didn't take it seriously, I would be humiliated in front of everyone, and I knew it too. For once, I took responsibility for myself and practiced the piece until I felt I had it down.

The night of the performance arrived, I stepped off of the bleachers and made my way to the microphone stand placed directly in front of the crowd. The music began; it was too late to pull out or run away. I closed my eyes, opened my mouth, and I fucking nailed it! When I opened my eyes again, everyone was on their feet and cheering. For the first time in my life, I felt seen and I finally understood that I could get the attention I craved through determination and hard work instead of bad behavior.

My senior year was drawing to a close in the late Spring of '77. Dad was traveling on business to Washington, DC and staying at a fancy, downtown hotel when he fell down a flight of 25 concrete steps after a night of heavy drinking. The following morning another guest found him lying in a pool of blood, unconscious, at the bottom of the stairwell. He was rushed by ambulance to the ER, where they drilled six holes into the top of his skull to alleviate the pressure from the bleeding in his brain. My mom received the call early Saturday morning and immediately jumped into the car, leaving Chris and me to fend for ourselves for the next two weeks.

She eventually returned home with my dad, who was for the most part, still unconscious. It wasn't safe for him to go up and down the stairs so he slept day and night on the couch we'd moved into the dining room. We were told, "If he doesn't improve and seems to be in great pain, call us immediately. That would mean the bleeding has worsened, and could mean clotting, which could kill him instantly." It got worse. It got much worse. It was terrifying to hear him moaning louder and louder in the middle of the night. Mom called the hospital to schedule his second brain surgery. This time, they cut a rectangular plate from the top of his skull and once they saw inside, they told her, "This guy has fallen many times before."

Their efforts still weren't enough and he began having regular grand mal seizures.[15] I'd been exposed to a lot of trauma as a child but nothing could have prepared me to witness my father stumbling through the house like an ogre, a monster, a big scary bear, bleeding out of the eyes and ears and hanging over the bathtub while convulsing and dripping blood.

He lost his driver's license and was placed on Federal Disability at the age of 53, so we sold the farmhouse and moved downtown to a large, white Victorian home in the quaint little borough of Lambertville; that way, my dad could get around without a car. It didn't take long before my mom decided she'd finally had enough and

---

[15] "Grand Mal Seizure" • A type of seizure involving loss of consciousness and violent muscle contractions.

moved to a one-bedroom apartment by herself, on the opposite side of town. She didn't take us kids; I was 18, my little brother Chris just 16, and only a sophomore in high school.

One terrifying night after Mom moved out and left us with him, I went to bed around 11 p.m. and woke up at 2:30 a.m. to hear my father stumbling up the stairs. He was hanging at the bar every evening, drinking heavily by then, even though the doctors told him it would kill him, "Kevin, any day you want to die, just take a drink." He was on several different prescription meds at the time to cut down on the frequency of his seizures, including Phenobarbital and Dilantin. Adding alcohol to that mix was extremely dangerous, but that didn't stop my dad. He was devastated by the loss of my mom, whom he adored, and the bar was his go-to in times of trouble.

I heard him fall hard in the bathroom and thought to myself, *"Fuck you, old man. I hope you die."* He had never paid much attention to me before and suddenly, I was completely responsible for him. I hated my mom for leaving me in charge of this crap.

"Mom, please… can we move in with you?"

"Oh, I guess so, but you'll have to sleep on the floor in a sleeping bag and you can't bring any of your stuff.

No thanks Mom, I got it. I'll clean up your mess. Chris came rushing into my room and I saw the fear in his innocent eyes.

"Help him! Please, I can't lift him."

I couldn't say no to my baby bro so I got up and walked to the bathroom to find that Dad had fallen again and was completely unconscious, bleeding from the back of the head. I called the Lambertville Rescue Squad and they came with a stretcher to take him to the hospital. We went back to bed for a couple of hours and Chris went to school that next morning like nothing had happened.

My dad was never the same again – not quite as bad as Jack Nicholson post-lobotomy in *One Flew Over the Cuckoo's Nest*, but not all there. He eventually recovered enough of his faculties to live on his own after my parents sold the house, but my father was a shell of his former self. He fantasized about winning the Irish Sweepstakes and buying a castle in Ireland to entertain the nobles. His one-bedroom apartment was stacked to the ceiling with boxes and boxes of Corelle dinnerware and he became what's commonly known as a hoarder. A hoarder with 5 cats. At least I was no longer afraid of him, and then one day, when I was about 24 years old, we hit a big milestone. He said something to me that allowed me to forgive him completely.

"I'm sorry I wasn't a good father to you when you were growing up, but I hope that you'll allow me to be any kind of father to you going forward," perfectly worded, totally honest, and straight from his heart.

OMG, he can see me! That gave me the power to choose what kind of relationship I wanted to have with him in the future. Every young woman should hear this from their emotionally absent dad. It was the single most healing moment of my life.

By then my mom was completely focused on her studies at Rutgers University. My father's accident left her without income, and at 42 she was too old to be a fashion model any longer; she needed money to live.

I had to get out of there; I thought I would implode from anger if I didn't. I registered for classes at Trenton State College because I knew as a New Jersey resident they would have to accept me. I applied for a 1% education loan from the state and added my name to the waiting list for a dorm.

I made a few good friends while at Trenton State but I never felt like I belonged there. Everyone else seemed to know what they wanted from life and how they intended to get it. Known as a "commuter school" at the time, many students went home for the weekend, but I had no home to go home to, so I stayed at the dorm with the one other girl who also had no home – smoking pot, playing backgammon, and listening to The Grateful Dead, Little Feat, Pure Prairie League, and all the great rock & roll records of the '70s. Music was always there for me. When no one cared, I could put on my James Taylor records to get back to baseline.

I was on my way to morbidly obese during this period of my life, and being high all the time, with a fully-stocked cafeteria downstairs wasn't helping me shed those pounds. I didn't know who I was or what I wanted to do. I was just biding my time, doing what I thought I was supposed to be doing but deep inside, I cried all the time. I changed majors every semester... Business Administration, Fashion Merchandising, Marketing, Theater... until I quit after just two years. Nothing was working for me so escape seemed the only conceivable solution.

3.
ESCAPE TO LOS ANGELES/ RADIO DAZE: 1979–1996

I wanted to run away from it all – college, my family, my reputation, the grotesque, overweight body I was living in, and the mean guys who teased me about it. "Hey, honey, you can't hide the fat under a skirt," a crowd of boys once yelled down to me from the roof of a Trenton State College dormitory. *How far away could I get? How far do I NEED to go?* I decided California was the place I oughta be, so I loaded up the truck and I moved to Beverly.[16] I convinced my friend Danny to come along with me. We packed our bags and took an AMTRAK train from Princeton Junction, NJ to Washington, DC, where we stayed with his oldest sister so we could fly out of Dulles Airport the following morning.

Our next destination was Pullman, WA, to live for the rest of the summer with his other sister, Marilyn and

---

[16] Paraphr. Henning, Paul. "The Ballad of Jed Clampett." *The Beverly Hillbillies.* Carolintone Music Company Inc. 1962.

her husband. We both got jobs grading papers for the University of Idaho, only 30 minutes from Pullman, and saved up enough money to purchase two Greyhound bus tickets from Spokane to Los Angeles. I will never forget the horrors I witnessed on that 3-day-and-night trip, stopping at all hours of the morning with homeless drug addicts lying all around the bus stations – the highlight being our 3 a.m. stop in Weed, CA; good for a photo op and at least one big laugh in an otherwise very scary experience.

Eventually, we landed in Hollywood and looked up to the hills to see the famed Hollywood sign peeking out from behind a dense cloud of smog. I instantly felt a sigh of relief come over me. *I'd finally made it.* I have a chance to move forward with my life without all the trauma from the past. I'm here to tell you, you CAN run away from your problems, at least for a while…

On our first night in Los Angeles, Danny and I stayed in a first-floor motel room, not realizing we were most likely being cased by the front desk worker and labeled as a couple of wide-eyed lambs, ripe for the picking. In the middle of the night, I woke to a sound coming from the outside, and opened only one eye a tiny sliver, to see a man removing the louvered glass panes from the window one by one, cutting through the screen with a knife, and climbing in to rob or maybe kill us. Danny didn't even wake up so I held my breath and pretended to be asleep too. I'd become quite adept at becoming invisible by then, and this time it served me well. He got away with $200 in Travelers Cheques and my prized leather backgammon set but thankfully, neither of us was hurt.

Danny's sister Marilyn set us up with a couple of entry-level jobs where she had formerly worked at M S Color Labs on North Cahuenga Boulevard in Hollywood. I was the company billing clerk, adding up invoices for photo reprints and enlargements, tapping away on my trusty paper calculator, stapling those invoices to the bags of photos, and placing them alphabetically out front in the bins for the customers to pick up. It was a good job; I loved my coworkers. Famous people came in all the time; John Derek was a regular there and occasionally brought along his wife Bo, or sometimes his former wife, Bond girl, Ursula Andress. The year was 1979, and the world was full of promise.

One day I was sitting in my tiny, windowless office and a coworker named Claire came in to ask a favor of me.

"My brother's band is receiving airplay on KROQ but every time I call in to request the song, they recognize my voice. Would you call them for me?"

"Sure Claire, sounds fun… whatever."

I called and the on-air DJ, Gary London, picked up the phone. I wasn't expecting that. I asked him to play the song and he remarked they'd had several requests earlier that day and agreed to play it for me later in his shift. As I was thanking him, the phone dropped to the floor, I heard a scurry of activity and then I overheard

Gary doing a live radio break. It was so cool to feel like an insider in that moment. He finished the break, picked the phone back up off the floor, and continued the conversation like nothing had happened and he didn't almost miss his cue. "What the heck was that there, sir?" I asked.

"Every now and again, the Program Director comes in and swings the tire tube, throws me a banana, and I perform."

Weird, okay, but you are in LA, Erin. The call stuck with me and the next week while I was shopping for groceries at the local Ralph's, to my surprise, they had little niños bananas neatly displayed in the produce section. I grabbed a small bunch, packed them up and mailed them off to Gary at KROQ as a thank you and guess what, he called! A big, LA radio jock calling me!

"I want to meet you. How about the next time I come into your lab to get my astronomy photos processed, I'll ask for you," and a week later he did just that. We began dating and I kept to myself that I was only 19 years old at the time, because he was almost 35 – an even wider age gap than my parents. Gary was like a dad to me. He was doting and a bit controlling and full of interesting facts to impart to a young, impressionable girl. I ate it all up.

I would work at the color lab by day, and because he was the evening DJ on KWST-FM from 10 p.m. to 2 a.m., I would go to work with him and hang out at the radio station. One day I asked him, "Hey Gary, how hard is it to be a DJ?" He joked, "Erin, a trained monkey could do this," and I thought to myself, *that's for me! Easy peasy; I'm an expert talker and I love rock & roll.* I took broadcasting classes in preparation to test for my First-Class Radiotelephone Operator license and passed the test on the very first try. Career path, set… "I am a DJ, I AM what I play."[17]

Bit by bit, I began to feel more comfortable in my skin and the pounds started to come off naturally. Danny had already left to go home and I was on my own in LA. Running away turned out to be one of the best decisions of my life and I believe it saved me, at least temporarily, from my own past.

204 pounds, 190 pounds, 175 pounds, and then 160. I was beginning to look like a normal, young girl and along with the weight loss, the cool rock & roll boyfriend, and just making it in LA did wonders for my self-esteem and my motivation to succeed. I had something to prove; I didn't know what it was, but it was something, and I could feel it was within my grasp.

Gary eventually moved to Fresno; he said LA had become too stressful for him. In truth, he had a pretty serious cocaine addiction and the temptation to use in LA was just too great. With Gary gone, I had extra time on my hands so I applied to be an intern at KWST. They were looking for someone to work in the News department to read the Bearcat scanner for the legendary Raechel Donahue, the preeminent female DJ in all of California. J.J. Jackson, of MTV fame, also worked there at the time,

---

[17] Bowie, David. "DJ." *Lodger.* Warner Chappell Music. 1979.

and one late night when I was pulling records for his shift, the AP ticker was unusually active. I walked over to the machine to see what was going on and read that John Lennon had just been shot. I ripped the feed off of the machine and ran it in to J.J. I watched that ticker all night and cried when I read that he'd died. That was a very sad day and it felt like the world was no longer full of promise.

I spent about six months at KWST, riding the elevator with a variety of wacky *Gong Show* and *Family Feud* contestants, and sometimes even the iconic producer/host Chuck Barris himself, who taped in the television studio upstairs from the radio station. Living in LA was a hoot; famous people and classic movie scenery were everywhere you turned. My next internship was for the World Famous KROQ in Pasadena where I landed a job as the receptionist and gopher[18] for the Sales department. I turned in gas receipts and made $50 cash per week. I would have paid them twice that much for all the fun experiences I had there, and the fascinating people I got to meet.

Working at KROQ was like running away with the circus. Every day there was a new cast of characters wandering around trying to get the attention of the DJs – would-be future rock stars like Nikki Sixx of Mötley Crüe dressed in a business suit, acting as manager/bassist; doing my makeup in the bathroom mirror standing next to punk

---

[18] "Gopher" • Known today as an "Intern," a "Gofer" (sic) was typically a young apprentice who, when not studying the trade, would run errands, i.e.: "Go fer this," "Go fer that," etc.

rocker Wendy O. Williams of the Plasmatics; Ricky Nelson and his kids hanging out in the on-air studio. A cast of characters the likes of which you've never seen, all in the same place together.

I loved watching the DJs work. I could spend hours sitting in the studio behind Jed the Fish, studying his timing and slip-cueing[19] techniques. I wanted to be the famed DJ Dusty Street and became best friends with another young DJ, April Whitney, who was the same age as me and already an LA radio superstar. April and I had crossed paths at the station; she was very friendly and super-gorgeous. Another gorgeous being was our production director, Ben Frances. I asked him to teach me how to use the editing equipment and he invited me to record some commercials and jingles for the station. *OMG, my voice is on KROQ!* Spending all that time together locked in a small production studio created a bit of friction, a sexual tension we could both feel. We began secretly dating. One day, while manning the front desk, I received a call from April.

"Hi Erin. I was doing my shift last night and I noticed a pink envelope smelling of perfume in Ben's message box. Do you know if he's seeing someone?"

I stated, "I'll be right over." I confessed to her that it was me and she laughed. No big deal, she just wanted to know;

---

[19] "Slip-cueing" • Turntable-based DJ technique of holding a record still while the platter rotates underneath the slipmat, releasing it at the right moment. Used by radio stations to match a following song to the preceding song, preserving the beat.

she was sort of seeing him too. Ben was a side hustle for both of us and we were both still involved with our *older* boyfriend/daddies, Chuck and Gary. Fast forward a few weeks and April and I got together for lunch.

"Ben took me to Trader Vic's Friday night. It was so much fun!"

"Really, April? He took me there Saturday night."

Uh oh. We talked some more and realized there was an unimaginative pattern happening here and decided that Ben was going to have to pay. We invited him out to dinner at our favorite restaurant, El Coyote, and seated ourselves on either side of him, wearing matching outfits and alternately feeding him chips and salsa while kissing his neck. After dinner, we all made our way downtown to the Revolving Lounge atop the Bonaventure Hotel.

"We're headed to the ladies' room to powder our noses. Please order us the most expensive bottle of champagne," and then proceeded down the escalator to a waiting cab and left him there with the bill and no 3-way that evening for poor Ben. He apologized to us both, laughed it off, and said that he deserved it. All three of us are great friends to this day.

One day Rick Carroll, our Program Director and creator of the popular Roq-of-the-80s format, invited me to do my first on-air shift. *I'd made it!* He had listened to my demo tapes and liked them enough to give me a shot. *I'm on my way!* My dream of being a radio DJ was finally coming true. I arrived at the studio after the legendary Rodney Bingenheimer's[20] Sunday night show and ran eight hours of prerecorded programming, only speaking at the top of each hour to give the call letters and dial frequency, but somehow, someway, someone important to my future was listening that night and he also liked what he heard.

On Monday morning, I was sitting in the lobby in front of the famed grass-cloth wall and the phone rang.

"Hi, my name is Jim. Can you tell me the name of the air personality who was on between midnight and 6 a.m. last night?"

"Why yes, it was me!"

"I'd like to offer you a job in Santa Barbara. I am the Program Director of KTYD-FM and we're looking for a new evening host; I think you'd be perfect. Can you drive up and meet me later this week?" *DUH. Of course!*

Santa Barbara was absolutely beautiful; who wouldn't want to live there? I became a full-time DJ at KTYD and my salary doubled to $100 a week. I made a name for myself, my ratings were excellent, and I was eventually moved to the coveted midday slot.

---

[20] "Rodney Bingenheimer" • Iconic, trendsetting DJ on the legendary, pioneer alt-rock radio station KROQ-FM, in Los Angeles from 1976-2016.

Many celebrities made their homes in the Santa Barbara/ Montecito area, including Mike Love of the Beach Boys. He owned a nonprofit on a 2.5-acre property overlooking the Pacific Ocean, affectionately known as the Love Compound – a small community of homes with tiny wooden and stained glass houses which they used to teach Transcendental Meditation[21] to like-minded people, many of them local musicians whom I'd met while working at KTYD.

Additionally, there was a recording studio on the property and I was invited to move in with five male musicians. I had my own private entrance and bedroom adjacent to the climate-controlled Beach Boys tape library. The property was perched high above the water, with rickety wooden steps leading down to the beach, exactly like the house on Cape Cod where I first dreamed of living by the ocean.

Over the two years I worked at KTYD, I met tons of legendary rock stars. Access to these artists was easy, and I got to interview people like Bryan Ferry, the hot guys of INXS, Nick Lowe, The Sex Pistols' Steve Jones, Joe Strummer of The Clash, and The Bangles before they were famous. Everything seemed to be flowing at that time in my life. I almost forgot where I came from because I was on my way to a better future, a future I had created for myself.

---

[21] "Transcendental Meditation" • Popularized by The Beatles in the 1960s. A form of silent mantra created by the Maharishi Mahesh Yogi in the mid-1950s. The technique is claimed to promote relaxed awareness, stress relief, and access to higher states of consciousness.

I'd heard that the 1982 *Billboard*[22] convention was going to be held in Pasadena, so I drove the 100 miles down the California coast to see my old friends at KROQ and hopefully meet some more bigwigs in the biz who could help me move forward in my new chosen career. Milling about the crowd, I overheard my idol, Dusty Street, speaking with Charlie Kendall, the Program Director of WMMR-FM in Philadelphia, who was trying to convince her to come work for him.

"It snows there, right? No way! You couldn't pay me enough."

I whispered in her ear, "Tell him to hire me, Dusty."

"They're out of your league, girlfriend," she scoffed.

Well, that's all anyone needs to say to me is, "You can't have it" and I'll show YOU; yes I can, and I will, thank you very much! I spent the next nine months courting Charlie long distance with weekly radio airchecks,[23] voicemails, marketing materials from promotions I was hosting in Santa Barbara, and the occasional postcard of palm trees waving, where I would write on the back, 'Wish I Was There,' instead of 'Wish You Were Here.' Ultimately it worked, and one day while laying out in the sun on my roof, I heard the message machine pop on and a familiar deep and resonant

---

[22] "*Billboard*" • The number one radio and record trade magazine at the time.

[23] "Aircheck" • A condensed recording of a DJ's show, usually combined with a resume in a job search package.

voice saying, "Hey you! It's Charlie. I just overnighted you a one-way plane ticket. Quit your job tonight. I'll see you in my office first thing Monday morning."

I played that message over and over again. I couldn't believe my ears. *Not out of my league, Dusty.* I quit my job that same day, flew back east, and was waiting on a bench in Philadelphia's Rittenhouse Square by 8 a.m. the following Monday morning. After what felt like several days, but was only two hours, I headed across the Square to the Wellington Building and pressed the elevator button for the 2nd floor.

Charlie invited me into his office, "I have good news and I have bad news," he said.

I felt my heart sink and a lump beginning to form in my throat.

"Which would you like to hear first?"

I sat frozen. He continued.

"Ok, on Friday I fired the night DJ, but the AFTRA[24] Union is demanding I pay out his contract and the station won't let me do it." *Is that the bad news or the good news? I was genuinely frightened. What if I had quit my job back in Santa Barbara but there was no job for me here?*

Charlie continued on while I held my breath.

---

[24] "AFTRA" • **American Federation of Television and Radio Artists**

"So, sorry honey, you're not going to be a DJ here, but the Music Director position is open and I'd like to offer it to you."

"But Charlie, I'm only 23 and I've never been a Music Director before."

He said confidently, "You'll be fine."

What choice did I have? Philadelphia, here I come. He was right; I was fine. I was better than fine. Landing a job like that for anyone was saying that you'd arrived. I'd jumped over several steps that others had to take on their way to the top. I was lucky and my self-perception began to change.

Being the MD of WMMR in the '80s was the dream job of a lifetime. The music business was experiencing an upswing due to the invention of CDs and promotional videos on MTV. Everyone was thriving and flush with money; the drugs flowed freely. Every Monday, each of the major record label execs and local promo guys (think Artie Fufkin from *This is Spinal Tap*) would call or wait in line to visit with me to promote their new records. On Tuesdays, I would select the very best new songs to introduce to the rest of the programming staff, and together, we all decided what to add to our regular rotation.

WMMR was the hottest rock & roll radio station in the country at that time; all eyes and ears were on what WE were playing. We were influencers and I was the front line. I was courted by artist managers, agents, and even the rock stars themselves. They were all fighting over who would take me to dinner, in a limo, to meet everyone from David Bowie to Bruce Springsteen. Backstage at concerts became routine. I wore the role well and never took for granted that I was privileged to have access to the musicians who'd molded my teen years.

James Taylor was coming to play at the Mann Music Center in Fairmount Park and I called my rep at Columbia Records to ask him a special favor. "I would like to meet James, all by myself, with no one else there. Can you make that happen?"

"Yes," he said, "For you, of course."

I waited after the show in a tiny backstage room for James to finish showering. He knocked on the door, entered the room, and sat down in a chair across from me. I mustered up all my courage and spoke the words I'd always wanted to say to him. "Thank you for always being there for me, when no one else was." I meant it, with all my heart. He looked down to the floor, somewhat shy, and let out a quiet sigh. I felt awkward. I thought he'd respond, so nervous me started filling up the vacant air with more words.

"I'm sorry, I hope I didn't say anything to make you uncomfortable." He looked up at me with those soulful brown eyes and calmly stated, "Erin, if someone hadn't said that to me at least once in my life, I'd wonder what the hell I'd been DOING all these years." We shared a laugh, and then he hugged me.

One famous rock star took particular notice of me and I have a hundred fun stories of hanging out with Steven Tyler and Aerosmith, my favorite one being the time midday DJ Pierre Robert and I greeted them at the Philadelphia Cargo airport with some listeners. As they deplaned to 50 cheering fans, Steven grabbed me by the arm and pulled me into the band's limo for the ride to the Spectrum, Philly's premier concert venue at that time. The problem was that I was carrying the portable broadcast system (called a "Marti") and had to conduct Pierre's interview for him live, on the air, with Steven and Joe in the limo. The Program Director was furious because I wasn't a full-time DJ. I almost got fired that day, but fortunately, I didn't. They knew the bands loved working with me because I truly cared. Just like Penny Lane in *Almost Famous*, I thought of myself as more of a Band-Aid – anything to be of help to others, like a good, codependent child of an alcoholic.

On the outside, everything was hunky-dory. I had my own apartment just a block from the station on Rittenhouse Square, and for the first time people seemed interested in what I had to say. On the inside though, nothing much had changed. One day, my office line rang and it was my buddy Jon Bon Jovi.

"Come to The Warehouse recording studio tonight, I have something I want to play for you."

I'd already had plans with our Program Director, Tom, to see the new version of Van Halen we jokingly referred to as "Van Hagar" and I told Jon that.

"You'll be out after three songs. It's just not the same without Dave."

He was right. Tom and I split after three songs and grabbed a cab down to Delaware Avenue to hear what Jon, Richie, and their engineer Obie were working on. Around midnight, Tom announced that he needed to catch the last SEPTA train home and we headed downstairs to hail a cab. The moment we stepped outside, he grabbed me by the shoulders, spun me around, pressed me up against the brick wall and kissed me, hard. I felt a lightning bolt travel right through my skull. *What the hell was that?* We began an affair under everyone's nose thinking we were so damn clever and secretive, but the entire world could feel the sexual energy that coursed between us.

It's never a good idea to fool around with your boss, but the bigger problem with Tom was that he was married, <u>very</u> married, and with two young children. We kept it under wraps for a very long time but we were acting crazy, sneaking around everywhere for well over a year. I think people knew but we denied it every time. Two years into our wild love affair, things were breaking down at home for him (no surprise) and he and his wife sought counseling.

The therapist told them, "If you want to repair your marriage, you'll have to come clean and tell her the truth." His wife, Sharon, asked him, "I need to know how many times you have been with Erin?" Tom thought about it for a minute or so and responded, matter-of-factly, "I don't know, about a hundred?" Well, that was just too much for any woman to bear and she tossed him out of the house. At first, we were both elated to be out in the open together, until my phone started ringing in the middle of the night, each and every night. I would wake up and pick it up, only to hear a dial tone. Her girlfriends would intentionally bump into me at parties whispering HOMEWRECKER into my ear.

Eventually, the calls died down and Tom and I became a real couple. He invited me to the island of Antigua to stay at his parents' family villa. His family spent their vacations there for many years, occasionally running into various rock stars who enjoyed the island's relaxed and familiar-feeling vibe. Antigua had been visited by Christopher Columbus in 1493 but it wasn't until British settlers arrived in 1632 when it became a colony, and remained so until declaring its independence in 1981.

English Harbour, with its crystal, clear Caribbean waters and pink sandy beaches, was the site of a restored British colonial naval station called Nelson's Dockyard. It was the place to hang, filled with casual pubs serving British-influenced fare like Bangers and Mash, Shepherd's Pie, and an array of hand-crafted stout beers. There was always a billiard table and a dartboard at the back of the room. English musicians felt at home here; you might run into Elton John or Eric Clapton, who eventually built his Crossroads rehab on the island. Keith Richards and his family stayed on the far side, in Dickenson Bay, near Tom's parents' place. There, he could go unrecognized and enjoy his time away with Patti, his young daughters

Teddy and Alex, along with big sister Angela, all frolicking on the beach.

"Hey, Erin, maybe we'll see Keith on this trip," grinned Tom, and no sooner did he say that when who, but Mr. Richards himself, hopped over the stone wall behind us, wearing – you guessed it – long, black swim trunks with big white skulls emblazoned all over them.

"'Ey Tommy-boy, mate! Good ter see yer, 'ow've yer been? Wanna play a game of quoits?"

Quoits is a pub game, much like horseshoes, but with doughnut-shaped, metal rings that you toss into a hole dug in the ground with a pin in the middle. Keith's makeshift version had us tossing the rings into coffee cans he'd buried in the sand.

"Ringer," Tom called out. "Nice one, Keith!"

"Shhh, don't call me Keith," Keith whispered loudly, "call me Sam."

"Uh, okay, Sam." *Wink.*

After the game ended, with 'Sam' winning, of course, he invited us to dinner later that evening.

"Me mate 'ere, Cha-lie, jus' opened a new pizza place in tahn, called Pizzas in Paradise.

Wanna join us, eh, luv?"

Duh, of course, we will.

"Arrighty then, we'll pick yer lads up at sev'n."

At 7 p.m. a tiny island car, with Keith at the wheel, pulled up to the house. Charlie was already in the passenger seat so Tom and I climbed into the back. We must have looked like a clown car; Tom is 6'2", his knees tucked up under his chin and Charlie, even taller.

"Before we go ea', do ya guys want to beehive ter Shirley 'eights and take in the view?"

By day, you can see the neighboring island of Montserrat from the highest point on the island and at night, it's like you are enveloped by a blanket of twinkling stars.

"Sure, let's go."

Keith could have driven us anywhere and we would have gone with him, he has such charisma, and he's a Rolling Stone! We climbed the windy road to the top and once we arrived, we all stepped out of the car to a dark, threatening cloud cover shrouding the stars. Keith lit up, as Keith always does, and passed the biggest blunt I'd ever seen to me.

"Lydies, first."

I took a hit and passed it to Tom, who passed it to Charlie, and round and round we went… Suddenly, there was a loud thunder crack, the sky opened up, and a downpour of rain drenched us, so we scrambled back into the car for the windy and now quite treacherous drive back down to the bottom.

Reeling from Keith's impossibly strong pot, I told Tom, "I need to go home, I'm too high." Tom pleaded with me, "But I want to have dinner with Keith." That's fine, just take me back to the villa first, *pleeease*. Keith turned the car around, dropped me off and I let myself in. *What was in that?* I wondered, or does Keith just get the best stuff money can buy?

Food, I need food, what's here? I rifled through the kitchen cabinets but they were completely bare. Nothing in the fridge either. I was desperate. I opened the freezer door to find an ancient package of Danish, frozen into the center of a block of ice. I grabbed a butter knife and proceeded to chip away, trying to dislodge them. I turned on the oven to warm it up while feverishly picking at the ice until it finally came loose. *Whew.*

I located a sheet pan, placed the 10-year-old, freezer-burned Danish on it, and opened the door of the stove; it was ice cold. *Oh damn, I'd forgotten to light the pilot!* I rummaged around for a pack of matches, found and lit one, not thinking about how the gas had already been on for 20 minutes. *BANG!* A massive fireball rolled right over my head, throwing me across the room! Suddenly, I was completely sober; no Danish required.

I lay there on the kitchen floor, my back against the wall, terrified, and sobbing. I heard a key turn in the door.

"Tom, help me," I whimpered. He ran to the kitchen, I told him what had just happened and he carried me to the shower and dumped a whole bottle of conditioner on top of my head, combing through the charred and broken hair that curled around my face. He was kind not to tell me that my eyebrows were gone too, as were my eyelashes. He was so loving, so nurturing, he carried me to bed where I slept in his arms all night.

At 9 a.m., we woke to someone knocking on the front door. *Who could that be?* I wondered as I came to life, "Don't answer it, please," but Tom opened it anyway and in strolled Keith, holding an acoustic guitar.

"'Ow's me pretty lydy, ta-day? Feelin' better?"

He smiled at me, not even noticing that my eyebrows were gone. I rushed to grab a bandana to cover my hairline, which was now two inches higher than it was the day before, and Keith casually sat down on the couch and began strumming. We drank Bloody Marys for breakfast and sang Bob Marley songs all morning and I laughed to myself about my crazy rock & roll life. We came home from a great trip overall, and shortly thereafter, Tom was relocated to our sister station in New York City. I remained at WMMR for another two years.

Tom may have been a cheater, but he never once did or said anything hurtful to me. We never had a single fight. He didn't love me, but we've remained the best of friends for 39 years and I am beyond grateful for our friendship. It was wrong of me to allow a relationship with my married boss to happen. If you're not driving your own life and allow others to take the wheel, you can go down some pretty treacherous roads.

Most American corporate environments are a patriarchy and the music business is no exception. It truly is a boys' club and I was always very careful to leave the party early. My male counterparts could stay out all night, doing mounds of cocaine with the rock stars and label reps, many of whom surpassed me on the way up the corporate ladder, fat with salaries and executive privilege. Decades later, when the #MeToo movement began, I would jokingly call it #MeTooThousand for the numerous times I felt threatened and victimized by some of my male colleagues. Still, I carried on, toughie that I am. I knew there were scores of people lined up to steal my job so I shut my trap and went along with it all. *It is what it is, Erin. You're lucky to be here. Don't complain.*

After a few years at WMMR, I'd become well-established as a national music influencer. "What does Erin think of that song?" the other radio programmers would ask. "We're not going to add it until she does." It was the first time in my life that people actually seemed interested in what I thought, that my opinions were valid and worthy of serious consideration.

In 1987, I received the Billboard Magazine Major Market Music Director of the Year Award so I decided, for the very first time, to go in and ask the station for a raise. I prepared my pitch, citing my awards, our through-the-roof ratings, my longevity there, the relationships I'd built with various label reps and artists that had benefited the station through exclusive promotions and interviews, and oh, what some of the boys there were making at the time, which was easily more than 10 times my annual salary.

I dressed in my most professional work attire, had a clipboard with me and everything. I was ready and confidently marched down the bowling alley (our term for the long, straight hallway that split WMMR's studios and offices right down the middle). The General Manager at the time invited me into his office and closed the door behind me. To give you a visual image of what I was faced with, he had a wide array of sexually inappropriate knickknacks all over his desk. Boob-shaped coffee mugs, wind-up jumping penises, mini gas station calendars featuring nude women on cars… you get the idea.

"What can I do for you, Erin?"

"Well, I'm glad you've asked. I am here to ask you for a merit raise, something over the cost of living increase we receive each year."

I proceeded to read him my list of accomplishments and when I finished I paused to look up inquisitively at him for a response. *He had to say yes, right? I never ask for anything. It's damn near impossible for me to ask for something, remember… I can do without; I'm tough; I can handle it; I am a good martyr, just like my mommy and my grandmommy programmed me to be.* He finally spoke.

"Sit on my face and we can talk about it."

I froze solid for what seemed like a whole minute, then leapt up from my chair, turned around, and made a beeline for the door to leave before the tears began to flow. The next thing I knew, I could feel his breath on my neck. He was directly behind me with his arms on either side of me and trapped me against the door.

"I was just kidding," he said.

I turned around and defiantly faced him, bent my knee, and kicked the door with my heel just as hard as I could until his assistant came over and opened it.

"This thing is always sticking and sometimes it even locks all by itself."

"Yes," I stammered, and scurried back down the bowling alley to my office to cry some really big tears. *Why hasn't anyone ever taught me how to stick up for myself? I earned that raise, and I deserved it.*

Tom and I eventually broke up. The distance between Philadelphia and New York was a contributing factor and he needed to spend any extra time he had available with his kids.

One fateful Monday morning in January of 1991, the new General Manager called me down to his office. I sat down and could feel that something was terribly wrong; he wouldn't look me directly in the eye. I held my breath and heard him say, "We don't know what it is you do around here so we're eliminating your position."

What? I've been here for eight years, and this is just occurring to you? I call bullshit, but in that moment I froze again, in complete shock. I couldn't even process what I was hearing. My heart sank to the ground and I felt a huge lump forming in my throat. I choked out the words, "Are you giving me two weeks' notice?"

He said curtly, "No, you can leave now."

I begged him, "Please don't make me clean out my office in front of my coworkers, please, please, let me move out tonight after everyone else is gone."

He replied without emotion, "Sorry, I can't do that."

I fled down the bowling alley with tears streaming down my face, to the former Program Director who was our consultant at the time, and pleaded with him to ask them if they would let me do it later that evening. He did; I left the station and returned later that evening, crying buckets while packing my boxes and filling them with nearly a decade of memories. *Who was I now, if not the girl with the great ears? What would become of me?*

Those years taught me so much. I learned how to handle myself with grace as a single woman in the business world, and overall, the years I spent at WMMR were the most valuable of my life, but they only placed a temporary Band-Aid on my childhood wounds. For the first time, I felt seen and heard; my opinions mattered, at least regarding musical trends and hit songs. The added attention from rock stars didn't hurt either, but I was still broken inside because it was never real and it only provided a temporary fix.

4.

FIRST MARRIAGE: JUNE 1990–SEPTEMBER 1996

After Tom and I broke up, I slid into a deep depression. I was living life on autopilot… wake, work, rest, sleep, wake, work, rest, sleep… but I couldn't shake the sadness I felt inside. I decided to try therapy, and once again the therapist was not much help. In reality, his suggestions were more detrimental to me than helpful. During one session, I jokingly asked him, "Hey, don't you have any cute doctor friends I could date?"

"No, no doctor friends," he said.

However, he did inappropriately suggest I might like another of his patients and thought we could be, at the very least, friends. I was willing to meet him. "If you get a call from Stephen, friend of Steve, that's him," the therapist said. Stephen, friend of Steve, called the very next day and we set a date to meet each other.

I remember opening the door to him for our first blind date and thinking to myself, *WOW! He looks exactly like*

Harrison Ford! This is going to be the best first date of my life! Tom? Tom who?

As it turned out, we did have a lot in common. We both grew up poor, city kids with an alcoholic opposite-sex parent, we were rock & roll music lovers, and bonus – he played the guitar – very well, I might add! I thought I'd died and gone to heaven.

The dating was fast and furious! Stephen was determined to lock me into a relationship as quickly as possible. What I didn't realize at the time was that he had taken one look at me, sized me up, and thought to himself, I need someone to help me with these three young kids of mine. She just bought her first house, and bonus – I can get backstage to meet rock stars too! Looking back, I can see the patterns of behavior I'd missed before. Predators pretend to be charming to get you where they want you, which is close enough to get access to what you have that they want.

Two weeks into our dating whirlwind, he brought me to a diner on Roosevelt Boulevard in Northeast Philadelphia, just a few miles away from where he'd grown up, to meet his kids. We all sat in a booth with Stephen and me on one side and Lori – 7, Seth – 6, and precious little Aubrey, only 3 years old, sitting directly across from us. They all stared up at me, wide-eyed and cute as little buttons. I was smitten from the start. I just love kids, and this night sealed the deal.

A month after our first date, I was turning 31. I stayed at Stephen's apartment the night before and when we woke up in the morning he told me that we would be spending the day downtown, hanging out and playing guitar with one of his friends. *Huh? What makes you think I want to watch you and your friend jam for my birthday?* I thought to myself. As usual, I just let it happen to me without a fight and we got into his car and headed down to Center City. All of a sudden, he pulled over and stopped the car right in the middle of 4th Street outside the entrance to the Bourse Building.

"GET OUT!"

"What?"

"Get out of the car!"

I thought he was mad about something, but then he smiled and said something else… "Open the glove box first." I opened it and found an all-day pass to my favorite day spa Toppers! So, I enjoyed a relaxing birthday of pampering, while he played guitar with his friend.

By the time he came back to pick me up, I was like melted butter. I'd have gone anywhere with anyone, but lucky me – I was going on a birthday adventure with my hot, new, and super-generous boyfriend.

First stop, my favorite restaurant in all of Philadelphia, the elegant and eclectic Astral Plane, on Lombard Street. I'd brought many rock stars to dine there. We were seated at a round table in the back room, the one with the tall, wicker Peacock chair/throne. One by one, the waiters and waitresses served us course after course, accompanied by a hand-drawn calligraphy love message, each one beautifully matted and framed. We finished up our meal, stepped outside, and what did I see but a white, stretch limo waiting to take us to the Tower Theater to see Jackson Browne perform. Stephen opened the car door for me and I saw several large vases filled with pink carnations, strewn about the back seat. *Way to go, new boyfriend! I think I'll keep you!* On the drive to Upper Darby, with WMMR playing on the limo's stereo, I suddenly heard my name coming from the speakers. Pierre Robert was dedicating a song to me from Stephen, for my birthday. *Swoon.* We arrived at the Tower, took our seats, and halfway through the performance, I heard my name again.

"I'd like to dedicate this next song to Erin Riley of WMMR. It's her birthday today," shouted Jackson Browne from the stage. "Let's all wish her a happy one," and the crowd applauded. Jackson began playing my favorite song of his, "For A Dancer." Stephen had somehow set that up too.

What hadn't he thought of? How did I get so lucky to find a man that loves me this much? Will every birthday with him be this awesome? I sure hope so. Dream guy. Lucky Erin. Pinch me.

I eventually learned that this is called love bombing,[25] and it's what human vultures do to lure their prey. Stephen was a master love bomber.

Six weeks into our dating whirlwind, I was hanging out at home, listening to music, when the phone rang.

"Are you home, honey?"

"Yes."

"Okay if I come over?"

"Sure."

I figured he was at his apartment in the Northeast and calculated the drive time, about half an hour. Two seconds later, my doorbell rang. *I wonder who that could be?* I opened the front door and found Stephen there on bended knee, holding a maroon velvet ring box, and wearing a big grin. He'd called me from the phone booth across the street. Surprise! He gently handed me the box and I slowly lifted the lid to find a white plastic, adjustable Barbie Dream Bride engagement ring. He had purchased the entire Barbie set, complete with necklace and tiara, just to get that ring. I smiled back at him, "Yes," I said, "with all my heart." I'd never been treated like that before, like a princess, and I hoped it would go on forever.

---

[25] "Love bombing" • Excessive and/or overwhelming levels of affection and adoration used by narcissists to develop and maintain control over another.

We were married after only five months of dating when he moved into my tiny rowhouse in the Fitler Square area of downtown Philadelphia. His three adorable kids came to stay with us every other weekend. I was cool with them. Did I mention I just love kids?

On the morning of the wedding, 30 of our closest friends and family members gathered at my home for coffee and breakfast. It was a rainy day and I was upset about it. Everyone told me not to make too much of it so I put on my happy face and hoped for the best. Just before we all headed out, my friend Dar asked if she could speak to me alone. I said, "Of course," and we went upstairs to the bedroom for privacy.

"Are you sure you want to do this?"

"Of course!"

"Because if it looks too good to be true, it probably is."

I reassured her that I was sure, and she left it at that.

We all then boarded a bus decorated with ribbons, streamers, and hand painted signs for the one-hour drive south on Route 95, to Elkton, MD. We were married at Oh! Marie's Flower Shop and Wedding Chapel, Home of the Famous Heart-Shaped Arch, surrounded by mannequins wearing pastel bridesmaids' dresses with a velvet Elvis painting propped in a chair in the front row. His kids rounded out the wedding party with his son, Seth in a mini-tuxedo, and his daughters both wearing handmade hot pink taffeta dresses and carrying white wicker baskets filled with rose petals.

On the ride home to Philadelphia, the sun broke through to reveal a beautiful double rainbow. I took it as a good sign.

Two weeks later, I received a letter from the IRS placing a $27,000 lien on my house to satisfy Stephen's past unpaid tax liability. He'd been skirting the IRS for years, living with his father after his first wife threw him out and left him for his best friend. He and his dad had the same name, with the same address, and that's how he was able to dodge them for four full years. As is often the case with addicts, they tell you just enough of the truth to get you to have empathy for them, and Stephen was no different.

"I haven't filed my taxes yet this year but I did file an extension so I still have time. It's no big deal; they owe *me* money so it's just a matter of getting around to it."

A partial truth, and in this case, what you don't know CAN hurt you. I was furious with him and made him borrow the money from his boss but I should have had the marriage annulled right then and there. We began to fight, his drinking escalated rapidly, and I came to learn that he'd been hiding that from me too. During the five months we dated before we were married, he would take me out for dinner and nurse a single drink all evening, then drop me off at my place only to head straight to a bar to get hammered with his buddies. Fancy dinners were all paid for in cash. Stephen would whip out a wad of bills and I would think to myself, *isn't he so responsible? He doesn't run up his credit cards, he pays his debts up front.* The cognitive dissonance runs strong in me, and I never realized what the truth was until I was in too deep, and it was far too late.

It was only six weeks after the wedding when I lost my beloved WMMR job. With more and more coming to light about the secrets my new husband had kept from me, I fell into the deepest depression of my entire life. I could barely lift myself off the couch for the next two years. I'd get up in time to watch Phil Donahue[26] at 9 a.m., then a bunch of random soap operas, until Oprah Winfrey came on at 4 p.m. This was no way to start a marriage, even a bad one. Stephen tried to be supportive but his dream of having a happy, employed, new mom for his kids was dashed. One day he came home with a paperback book, *What Color is Your Parachute?* to help me discover a new career for myself, but I didn't want a new career; I wanted my old job back or at least something comparable.

I knew the real reason I was fired. It was because of my relationship with Tom. The powers that be had decided that one of us had to go and that one of us was a recently married woman.

---

[26] "Phil Donahue" • The pioneer of Daytime Talk TV from 1967 to 1996. *Donahue* was the first talk show to include audience participation.

"She'll be fine," they told themselves. "Her new husband will take care of her."

But I was not fine. I began to see the real Stephen – "Who do you think you are? You're not special. When I was out of work, I took a job at a local school cafeteria placing a banana on each plate. You think you're above that, don't you? Well, you're not. We need money and you need to get a job, now!" *What happened to the perfect man I thought I'd married?*

I applied at every other radio station in the market but no one in Philadelphia would hire me and I couldn't relocate because of his kids so I concocted another idea. *I'd have a baby.* I'd always wanted one and Stephen said he'd like to have another. He told me he wanted to do it "right" this time, with both parents together, so I stopped taking my birth control pills and was pregnant in no time. He was angry that I had timed the pregnancy by myself and he was right; it wasn't fair of me to go off the pill without telling him. *I'm sorry Stephen. I'm not perfect.*

Around this time the manager of Aerosmith called offering me a job on the road with the band doing the "meet and greets" for fans and local food bank promotions in each market on the tour. Unfortunately, I couldn't accept it because I was already pregnant.

Our son, Julian, named for my father, was born in July of 1992 and I was thrilled to be a stay-at-home mom until I was a stay-at-home mom in the winter. Like my mother, I had no role model for 'typical mom' and never felt comfortable in mommy groups talking about how many diapers my son had soiled that day, so Julian and I spent most of our days alone.

The two-bedroom, Trinity-style house[27] I owned on Locust Street was just too small for the six of us, so Stephen rented a three-bedroom house in Glenside, PA in a 1950s development, with a big yard where the kids could play. If only we'd felt like an actual family, but the move turned out to be just another Band-Aid, a temporary fix.

The problem was really Stephen's drinking. He spent a couple of evenings each week hanging out at the local bar on trivia nights while I stayed home with the baby. Sometimes he would fall asleep on the living room floor with the kids lying on his chest. I would wake up in the middle of the night to find them all in a pile on the rug with pornographic movies playing behind them on the TV. Whatever movie they'd been watching had ended hours before and HBO's programming had turned to adult content.

One by one, I would walk them or carry the smaller ones to their beds, go back to bed by myself and leave Stephen lying there on the floor. My resentment was growing and our fights about alcohol were daily. He tried to quit by buying only non-alcoholic beer. I tried to explain to

---

[27] "Trinity-Style House" • Typically a three- or four-story townhouse with each floor containing only one room. They were usually less than 1000 square feet total.

him that there's still a trace amount of alcohol in each one and if you drink 24 of them in a single afternoon, it's equivalent to a regular six-pack. That didn't change a thing. I've learned an addict must walk their own path out of addiction and no one can make them do it before they are ready. Stephen was not quite ready yet but the marriage was breaking at the seams.

He got a new job in Reading, PA, and suggested we move closer to cut down on his commute.

"I'm not willing to move any farther from the city than King of Prussia," I told him.

"We can't afford anything there, that's the Main Line."[28] I'd never been to any of the residential neighborhoods surrounding King of Prussia; I'd only shopped at the mall. I didn't know not to believe him and I still hadn't realized our relationship was based on a bunch of lies he told me, and that I then repeated to myself. The red flags were flying before we even met. What therapist acts like a dating matchmaker for his patients? I chose not to see them because I wanted the relationship to move forward. *If Tom didn't want me, at least someone did*, I told myself, and with blinders on, I proceeded right down the aisle straight into a special kind of hell.

---

[28] "The Main Line" • An affluent suburban area northwest of Philadelphia named after the once prestigious main line of the Pennsylvania Railroad.

Rather than fight back, we moved to Downingtown, a 45-minute commute for him but two hours to Philly for me. It was always what HE wanted, never what I wanted. He made more money than I did so he got the new car and I got a junker. He always had a brand-new cell phone and said that I didn't need one because I was home with the baby most days. One day, when I was picking Julian up from daycare in Glenside, that junker broke down. I found myself knocking on door after door with a baby on my hip, hoping to find someone at home so I could ask to use their phone and call for assistance. Gratefully, it was still light out and I was in a safe neighborhood when it happened, but I was scared nonetheless. I imagined being invited in to wait for help and being raped or murdered or maybe even held prisoner with Julian abducted and taken to another state. *Yikes, Erin, your trauma brain!*

A nice, elderly man came to the third door I knocked on and invited us in. He seemed too old and weak to hurt anyone, so I cautiously entered his home, sat down at the kitchen table, and called Stephen to come pick us up. When we arrived back at our house, I asked him again, "I was afraid something like this would happen. Can I please get a cell phone now?" Stephen did not respond. He turned and walked away from me, climbed the stairs up to the attic over our garage, and came back down with a 10-year-old briefcase phone.

"Here's your cell phone. It doesn't have a plan, but it works," as he handed over this huge, heavy thing. I never felt less cared for in my life than I did in that moment.

Gradually, our marriage eroded but I frantically kept trying. "Hey Stephen, the kids and I are watching a movie, would you like to join us?" No response. "Did you hear me?"

"I thought I heard a fly buzzing," he would say.

Ouch. I never understood why he was so mean toward me. I was only trying to make a happy family out of a toxic mess. Again.

The kids were only with us every other weekend, and they woke up very early, around 6:30 a.m. Somebody needed to be an actual parent to them and do the dirty work so, good ol' codependent me took on the job of fixing their breakfast and bathing them while Disneyland Dad would sleep in until 10:30 a.m. By the time he emerged from the bedroom, had his meal, and showered, I was already making lunch for myself and the kids. Eventually, we'd get out the door for an activity around 1 or 2 p.m. God forbid, I ask for any help from him because the answer was always, "I worked all week."

On Sunday evenings, Stephen would bring them back to their mom and step-dad's house in Northeast Philadelphia. He volunteered to do all the driving so his ex wouldn't see what a nice house we lived in, and start hitting him up for more child support. I should have known right then and there that it was never about what was best for his kids; it was always what was best for him.

I would eventually be treated the same way. He even went so far as to buy a brand-new SUV, an exact replica of his previous SUV, the same color and everything, but this one without a sunroof, in the hopes I wouldn't figure out that he'd bought yet another new car for himself. *Hide, lie, cheat, steal, hide, lie, cheat, steal.* And it wasn't just me; he "helped himself" to money from Julian's bank account and "borrowed" the small gifts of cash from the children's birthday cards! *Who does that?*

Whenever he would leave to drive them home, I would run around the house like a tornado, cleaning, trying to regain some sense of control over my space, over my life. When he returned one Sunday after I'd spent over two hours cleaning and picking up a weekend's worth of wet towels from four kids and a husband, I bemoaned, "How come none of your kids knows how to hang a towel?"

"You're the only one who cares," he quipped.

Ouch, yeah, pretty mean and insensitive but since I'm not one to stand up for myself and Stephen knew it, I once again rationalized that he was right so it became my job to do all the cleaning because I was the only one who cared.

My disappointment with my marriage grew and I began to think about leaving him. I knew if I did, I would need to find a full-time job to support myself and our son. On the morning of January 6, 1996, Stephen left for work in what would turn out to be one of the largest, record-breaking snowstorms the area had ever seen. Over two feet of snow fell that day and Julian and I were trapped inside the house alone for the next three days. It was a metaphor for how trapped I felt in an abusive and neglectful marriage to an addict, and the catalyst it took for me to make the decision to finally leave him.

We entered therapy together and I worked up the courage to tell him I wanted a divorce. Stephen didn't want the marriage to end but he knew there was no way to keep me after all we'd been through so he reluctantly gave me $10,000 to put a down payment on a little rowhouse in Manayunk, with parquet floors and two white pillars on either side of the living room. Manayunk was a hip and happening area just eight miles west of downtown Philadelphia. What I didn't know at the time was that his employer had just awarded him a huge number of stock options, which he chose to keep a secret from me. I also learned how vindictive he could be.

"If you don't want me, you can never see my kids again!"

His kids meant the world to me. I didn't want to leave them, I only wanted to leave him. This is known as triangulation,[29] and I would come to know this narcissistic tactic intimately during my second marriage.

––––––––

[29] "Triangulation" • A form of manipulation describing an insecure person's use of exclusionary threats to divide and control two or more people. The use of indirect communication, often behind someone's back, is the typical method.

I moved out and left Julian behind with Stephen. I convinced myself he'd be better off staying in a familiar home, maintaining the status quo, and not disrupting his young life. He was just four years old at the time and had been spending weekdays with his nanny, Jean, while Stephen drove to work in Reading and I to Center City Philadelphia for my new job as the regional Executive Director for the GRAMMY® organization. It was around this time that Stephen finally quit drinking for good, and I wanted more than anything for Julian to have a sober dad.

I reassured myself that if Stephen had to come home to relieve Jean every day after work, he wouldn't be able to stop at a bar, and maybe he could stay sober this time. It occurred to me much later in life that I had done exactly what my mother had done to my brother and me – abandoning my son and justifying to myself it was best. Sure, I visited him in Downingtown every Wednesday evening and brought him back to my new house every weekend, but Julian missed me terribly and begged to stay in Manayunk every Sunday night.

Stephen agreed it was in Julian's best interest to stay in Downingtown until he was ready to start school the following September, at which time he would move to Manayunk to live with me. When the time came to register him for school, I emailed Stephen proposing some different options and he wrote back, "He's not going anywhere. You left him. That's called abandonment and possession is nine-tenths of the law." I took that email directly to family court in West Chester and they scheduled a hearing. I was glad I had it all in writing, making it simple for the court to write an order saying Julian would come live with me and attend a private Quaker Friends school[30] in Philadelphia.

For a while, things seemed to settle down. Stephen and I eventually became friends and Julian enjoyed dinners and the occasional day trip with his parents and siblings.

I was never taught how to choose an appropriate partner, so I let them all choose me. Whoever showed up with the shiniest jewels and the most compliments were the ones who grabbed my attention, but all that glitters is NOT gold. No one ever taught me that there are predators out there pretending to be honest and trustworthy and that it was naïve of me to think everyone thought as I did, that people are inherently good, with empathy for others, and adhere to the golden rule. Just like a spider spinning a web to catch its prey. *Aren't those glistening webs mesmerizing? How can you not fly directly into one?*

---

[30] "Quaker Friends school" • These schools provide an academically sound education while also instilling Quaker values of community, spirituality, responsibility, and stewardship in their students.

5.

WXPN AND THE GRAMMYS: 1992–1996

Before leaving my first marriage, I'd been trying desperately to break back into the radio biz and applied to the nonprofit station owned by the University of Pennsylvania, WXPN-FM. Blues maestro Jonny Meister hired me to be the audio engineer for the station's award-winning children's program, *Kids Corner*. It was a way back in so I accepted it, and I did a terrible job. I'd been so unhappy at home, depressed, and distracted; I missed important cues, and one night the host Kathy stormed in and fired me on the spot. A week later, I ran into her in the hallway and she brusquely said, "No, you can't have your job back."

I didn't want it back. I thanked her for firing me; it was the wake-up call I needed. I made an appointment to speak with the General Manager and asked if there was anything else I could do at the station. He thought about it for a minute and came up with an idea. "Would you be interested in doing a national marketing project for *World Cafe*?" their very well-respected and nationally syndicated radio show. Now, this was more my speed and I set about calling music retail outlets all over the country to encourage them to feature the compilation CDs that *World Cafe* was releasing. *Slam dunk.* I succeeded and they gave me more to do.

"Can you produce this year's Singer Songwriter Weekend?"

Can I? Now here was a project I could really sink my teeth into. I still had plenty of contacts in the music biz and no one ever said no to WXPN. They'd broken so many influential artists over the years that everyone who could, would be willing to play a show for them for free. *Easy peasy, Erin. You can do this.* I was given a budget of only $5,000 and asked to create a two-day event with nine bands for 20,000 listeners. Shawn Colvin, Sarah McLachlan, T-Bone Burnett, Sonia Dada, The Subdudes, Iris Dement, John Gorka, October Project, Sam Phillips – a veritable who's who of the mid-'90s alternative music scene – all agreed to perform.

When it was over, I received a letter from the University's Office of the Vice-Provost congratulating me on earning over $20,000 for the station with only a small budget to work with. They asked me to do it again the following year, and that year we featured BoDeans, Paula Cole, Susan Werner, Black 47, Ani DiFranco, Wanderlust, Freedy Johnston, Patty Larkin, Jill Sobule, David Wilcox, and Patsy Foster. Another slam dunk!

I was really proud of myself; I had done such a good job for them. They took my resume and designed a full-time job, just for me. I felt myself coming back to life.

Living in my adorable rowhouse in Manayunk was a blast; just outside of downtown Philadelphia, teaming with attractive young people roaming the streets, shopping at the quaint little boutiques, and frequenting its many bars. I was 36 years old at the time, and my midlife crisis was in full swing.

I leased a rag-top Jeep Wrangler, began dating the 27-year-old car salesman who sold it to me, escaping all my parental responsibilities, and telling myself that Julian would be living with me again soon and entering Kindergarten. I had two very best friends who were living there at the same time and boy did we make a lot of great memories together – hanging at the bars, seeing all the local bands, and drinking several nights a week. My codependency showed up this time as enabling my one friend to drink too much. I bailed her out of several bad situations that I shouldn't have. Man, I had no idea I was so screwed up!

I never accepted the full-time job WXPN offered me. It only paid $24,000 a year and I knew I couldn't take care of myself on that little income. Through the grapevine, I heard about a job opening with The Recording Academy®, the organization that produces the annual GRAMMY Awards. I called the Trustee of the local chapter, Joe Tarsia, who was the owner of the legendary

Sigma Sound Studios[31] that produced many of the Philly soul hits of the '70s. We'd met at a live broadcast I'd produced for WMMR in the '80s, featuring Robert Fripp[32] and his League of Crafty Guitarists. Joe and I had always hit it off; he was a stand-up guy and I trusted him completely. He thought I'd be a great Executive Director and recommended that I be interviewed for the position.

The national team flew out to meet me and invited both Joe and the local chapter president, Marc, to come along for what ended up being a grueling, two-hour long interview. I must have done well because they called the very next day to schedule a second interview with me the following week. This one was to be held at the local chapter office on Broad Street.

When I arrived and entered the conference room, I looked up to find the entire 14-member Board of Governors staring back at me. One by one, each of them asked me questions about what I felt I could bring to the local chapter. I must have done well again because the very next day I was offered the job, a prestigious position held by only 12 other people around the country. It paid $36,000, a fortune to me at that time, so I immediately accepted it. Life was great.

---

[31] "Sigma Sound Studios" • Legendary recording studio established in 1968 by Joseph Tarsia. Known worldwide for its distinctive sound and recording innovations. Hits by the O'Jays, Stylistics, and others created "The Sound of Philadelphia," and drew top recording artists Stevie Wonder and David Bowie.

[32] "Robert Fripp" • Pioneer of the early 1970s Progressive Rock movement, most notably with his band King Crimson.

It was early February 1996 when I was hired and I hit the ground running, planning professional education events for area musicians and paid members of the organization. Only three weeks into the job, they flew me out to Los Angeles and put me up in a very fancy hotel for "GRAMMY Week" so I could attend the many black-tie events and activities leading up to the 38th Annual GRAMMY Awards at the Shrine Auditorium.

My first formal event was the Nominees' Party, always held the night prior to the telecast. I entered the lobby of the hotel and looked around to see crowds of music luminaries and high-profile record executives, with silver trays of butlered hors d'oeuvres being passed around, carved-ice sculptures spewing streams of champagne, and a gorgeous, long-haired naked woman playing the harp at the top of the escalator. I was in complete awe.

Stepping onto the escalator to the lower level, where all the action was, another Executive Director introduced herself. She was a pretty blond Texas gal with a fetching smile. She whispered to me, "Be careful, watch yourself, there are wolves here." *Hmm.* I wondered what she meant by that, but I would soon come to know that misogyny is not only pervasive in the commercial music industry, it is also quite prevalent in the nonprofit music world.

Stories of corruption and sexual harassment plagued the GRAMMY President at the time, and it eventually took him down, but not before I came to know coercive control at work, and not just at home.

After three-and-a-half years, I'd run my course with the GRAMMY organization and moved on to work at a popular Philadelphia repertory theater as Director of Marketing & Advertising. Turned out it wasn't a good fit for me and I missed being involved in music. They soon brought in a brand-new General Manager who made it crystal clear she was not a fan of mine and we both agreed to part ways. It was at this time that I met my second husband, Fabio.

6.

AWKWARD FIRST DATE: SEPTEMBER 1999

We met on Match.com and after a couple of weeks of exchanging emails, decided to meet "IRL" (in real life). Fabio drove to Philly and we met at The Wilma Theater where I was working at the time. The receptionist buzzed my extension to let me know I had a guest in the lobby so I asked a coworker to take a peek and see if he looked like his picture. He did, so I came out to say, "Hi. Gimme a minute." I went back to my desk, grabbed my purse, and back to the lobby I went. He stood up and followed me down the back stairs of the theater to Spruce Street where we caught a whiff of marijuana in the air and shared a secret smile... that question out of the way. *Wink.*

I took him around the corner to Shiroi Hana, my favorite sushi restaurant in town, and we sat at a table for two, directly across from each other. I ordered an assortment of my favorite sushi delicacies and after ten minutes of studying the menu, Fabio ordered three orders of fatty tuna, which I thought a bit odd.

He proceeded to ask me lots of questions about myself and was very attentive to my responses. I didn't realize I was being studied, like the menu; I assumed he was interested in getting to know who I was.

The waiter brought our lunch to the table and I proceeded to devour my sushi while answering his questions until I looked at his plate and noticed he hadn't even touched his yet. I said, "Aren't you going to eat your sushi?" He replied nonchalantly, "I had a big breakfast." I thought that odd as well but dismissed it immediately as I was enjoying the attention. He never once touched his sushi in two hours and when the waiter came to take our plates away he paid the check and I brought him back over to the Wilma to give him a tour of the theater.

While showing him around, the box office manager ran up to me, yelling "Where have you been? The system is down, nothing is working, we can't sell any tickets!" The box office was my responsibility and all its staff members reported to me so I was listening intently trying to diagnose the problem. When I turned around to tell Fabio I needed to cut the date short he was nowhere to be found. He'd just vanished into thin air without so much as a tap on the shoulder or a goodbye.

I headed home after work that evening, thinking he just didn't like me and disappearing was his way to escape our date, but when I arrived home there was a message from him saying he really enjoyed our time together and wanted to see me again. I dismissed his awkwardness and shoved down the feelings of discomfort I felt with him because I was just so happy to be wrong and hear that he liked me.

This guy was different from anyone I'd dated before so I decided to give him a try. Clearly, I had no idea how to choose a good relationship so maybe I'd been wrong all along and the perfect partner for me would be the strong, silent type; *maybe there would be less conflict,* I told myself. Little did I know, I'd allowed a narcissist into my life, but this one was dressed in sheep's clothing.

I called my friend Dar, who worked at the same company that he did – R.O.U.S Industries – and asked her if she knew him.

She said, "Sure, he fixes my computer when I have trouble."

"What do you think of him?" I asked.

She paused and said, "He's okay, I guess, but joyless." *Hmm, another thing for Erin to do. I'm Birdie, I can make him happy.* I love a project.

7.

DATING/MIRRORING[33]/ LOVE BOMBING: 1999-2001

While our first date was a bit awkward, our second and third dates were rather nice. For date number two, we enjoyed a delicious meal at a local Afro-Cuban restaurant in Manayunk, where I'd been living for the past three years. He walked me home and kissed me goodnight; it was a very nice kiss and I felt the attraction.

Everything seemed to be progressing normally, so for our third date, I invited him to my home for dinner and to watch my favorite movie. I made a vegetable lasagna, with fresh veggies from my backyard garden, not aware yet that Fabio didn't *eat* vegetables. He faked it pretty well, trying to make a good impression as a well-rounded guy, who liked the same things I did. I was completely unaware that I was being *mirrored* by

---

[33] "Mirroring" • A narcissist will pretend to hold the same interests and/or beliefs as their target as a means by which to gain entry into their life.

a master manipulator, and next up would be his most masterful trick.

I must have mentioned to him at lunch that *The Princess Bride* was my very favorite movie of all time (but forgotten I'd done so). Either that, or it was listed on my Match.com profile. After dinner, I was excited to share it with him so I popped the VHS tape into the slot and as the opening strains of Mark Knopfler's "Storybook Love" began to swell, Fabio proceeded to recite every single word to the intro of the movie.

I thought I'd died and gone to heaven! *I've met my perfect man! What other man would know all the words to my favorite movie?* I took it as a sign but I should have seen it as a big red flag. They call this mirroring, matching up with everything that matters to you, whether it's true or not. It is for a purpose, a means to an end.

We'd spent summers competing on our local swim teams; we were lifeguards too. We both loved the beach and preferred the warmer weather. He shared my musical tastes, a love of classic rock bands that would take us to dozens of concerts together over the next 20 years. Politically, he identified as liberal, he was a former hippie, and pot smoker, just like me. He didn't waste his weekends watching football on the couch with a beer in hand; he liked to work hard, renovating the house. I, too, loved home renovation, ever since my parents purchased the old stone farmhouse outside of Lambertville. I imagined how great our relationship could be.

He was an attentive boyfriend. He drove two hours to and from work every weekday, stopped home to feed his dog, and then drove over to my house to spend time with me. Flowers every date, and one time, a Tiffany cuff bracelet, for no reason at all. When Hurricane Floyd blew a corner of the roof off my rowhouse, he climbed up there and fixed it all by himself. My hero.

I made him wait six whole weeks before having sex with him. He was the perfect gentleman and didn't pressure me at all. One night he came over after work, I was finally ready, and I let him know.

He was so nervous, he couldn't even look me in the eye. He made absolutely no sounds, looked over my shoulder the entire time, and held his breath. I asked him if he enjoyed himself because he gave no outward indication. He told me that he did and he hadn't made a sound because he was trying to last as long as possible. It seemed a plausible reason, to my rational-thinking brain.

I thought I could bring him out of his shell and help him build confidence sexually. I remember thinking to myself, *this guy will never cheat, he's too shy.* I had no idea at the time but that night should have been the biggest red flag of all. Instead, I excused it away and thought I could "fix" it. *Woohoo, another project for Erin.* In the end, it was all about sex, power, and control, and his need for me to heal what happened to him during his teen years while in high school. I didn't know what I'd gotten myself into yet.

Things quickly turned when one day, we were hanging out at his rented bachelor pad in Chesterfield Woods when suddenly, his 12-year-old daughter, Layla, came bursting through the front door, dropped off by her mom with no advance notice. I was sitting on the couch in the living room with my back to the door and spun around when I heard the door burst open and our eyes met. She froze. I smiled at her and she screamed, "Daddy! Get her out of here, make her go away!" then ran upstairs crying and slammed her bedroom door shut.

Fabio whispered, "I'd better go get her."

I said, "Sure."

Thirty minutes later he came back downstairs without her and asked me if I wouldn't mind leaving. I left and this was my very first mistake in what would become the triangulation of her and me that went on for the next 18 years.

Fabio's relationship with his daughter Layla was clearly unusual and sometimes altogether inappropriate. He would come downstairs to make coffee in the morning completely naked in front of her. I thought I could help him become a more tuned-in and better parent by gently guiding him.

"Fabio, you can't parade around naked in front of your 12-year-old daughter. She's a developing young girl and it's confusing to her."

He responded, "Well, I don't want her to feel self-conscious and ashamed of her body."

I questioned him, "Did your parents walk around the house naked in front of you?"

"No."

"Are you self-conscious and ashamed of your body?"

"No."

He would barge in on her in the bathroom while she was bathing, and I saw her cover her chest and curl up in a ball in the bathtub. *Hmmm.* More weird stuff for Erin to fix. *I just need to get through to him.*

Little by little, confusing statements began to come from him. He alluded to having lunch with a female coworker a couple of weeks prior. I recalled having heard her name before and asked, "Isn't that the married woman you had an affair with and thought she was 'The One'?"

"Yes."

"Why did you not tell me?"

"I didn't NOT tell you."

My crazy brain leapt into action, *he must mean that he wasn't intentionally keeping it from me because there was nothing to hide.* I now realize that he said that to deliberately confuse me and this was to happen again and again over the many years we spent together. I failed that test, or actually, passed it in the eyes of a narc.[34] My lack of response or pushback showed him I was easily manipulated and would back down, rather than confront him. This is what's called word salad[35] and it is the beginning of coercive control.[36]

We'd been dating for about four months and it was now February 2000. Things were progressing along, I was ignoring all the red flags, so we planned our first vacation together to Oahu, where I tested for and received my PADI[37] Open Water Diver certification. Fabio was an expert diver, certified since high school, and we were both thrilled that I passed easily in the rough waves of the challenging North Shore. We could now travel and dive all over the world together.

On the way to Hawaii we stayed in Los Angeles to attend the 42nd Annual GRAMMY Awards at the Staples Center – you know, the one where JLo wore that green dress everyone could see from any seat in the house. I was excited to bring him to the

---

[34] "Narc" • Abbreviation of "Narcissist."

[35] "'Narcissistic' Word Salad" • A type of purposefully confusing speech using circular reasoning, logical fallacies, and other rhetorical devices to disorient and manipulate a person. Narcissists use it in gaslighting their targets.

[36] "Coercive Control" • A form of domestic abuse or intimate partner violence describing behaviors a perpetrator uses to gain control and power by eroding a person's autonomy and self-esteem.

[37] "PADI" • Professional Association of Diving Instructors

after-parties and show off my hot new man to all my former coworkers.

After the show, we headed to the Biltmore Hotel and proceeded to stroll arm in arm down the wide, center hallway, checking out the scene. GRAMMY parties are very lavish. Every party room along the hall features a variety of delectable and upscale catering, representing some of the most expensive and best-known restaurants from around Los Angeles. There are ice fountains spewing champagne with bartenders mixing cocktails and lots of celebrities in attendance. Live bands playing music of all styles spill out into the hall from every room. It's impossible to decide what to check out first; everything is so inviting and luxurious.

One room, in particular, was calling my name and I grabbed Fabio's arm and dragged him in to watch the legendary Bar-Kays performing. Everyone was on their feet dancing. I pulled him onto the dance floor and he just stood there, looking uncomfortable, with his arms at his sides. I asked, "Aren't you going to dance with me?"

"I don't dance," he said, expressionless.

I looked at him, puzzled.

"Cool guys don't dance," was Fabio's response, deadpan.

Huh? This new man of mine sure was perplexing; but to me it was just another sign that over time, and with a little encouragement, he would feel more and more at ease with me, loosen up, and perhaps I could get him to dance. *You can fix this too, Erin.* I didn't realize at the time that he was setting the stage to be Joe Cool, so I would have low expectations of him.

I would rationalize to myself, he's my tall, dark, handsome, strong, silent type – protector. That's how I would describe him to all my friends. Since I don't know how to choose the right man, he made it easy for me, by making it crystal clear that he had chosen me.

Around this time, my first husband bought a sweet, little three-bedroom rancher with a yard, just a few miles away. One Friday evening, when I was dropping Julian off for his weekend visitation, I walked into the house to find a brand-new, fully renovated kitchen complete with stainless steel appliances and granite countertops. "Wow, Stephen, where'd you get the money to do all of this?" I inquired.

"I have $600,000 in the bank and I can buy any house I want," he boasted.

I remember thinking to myself, *how do you have $600,000 in the bank when I only have $40?* I got into my car and drove over to Fabio's condo to spend the weekend and told him what had just happened.

He said, "Looks like you're due for a raise in child support. Why don't you ask him for a current pay stub or tax return?"

Up until then, Stephen had been paying me $600 a month, an amount determined by him, and I just didn't want to make any waves by asking for more. I already felt guilty for leaving him and it was just enough to subsidize the income from my GRAMMY job. On Sunday evening, when I picked up Julian, I asked Stephen to provide a recent tax return.

His emphatic response: "No."

Really? No? Just like that, no? I don't think you can do that. I asked Fabio what he thought and he explained that all I needed to do was go to the local domestic relations office and file a complaint. They would subpoena his current income info for me, so I did just that... and Stephen punished me for it in court for the next three years.

It turned out he had liquidated that considerable stock package granted to him by his employer in June of 1996, which was now worth about a million dollars. *That's how the kitchen. That's how the boat. That's how all the vacations. Hmmm.* This stock was awarded to him while we were still married, and therefore should have been a marital asset, but he had kept it a secret from me.

The court more than tripled my monthly child support and Stephen was absolutely furious. He fought it tooth and nail, to the death it seemed. He had only been paying $600 a month to his first wife who divorced him, for their three kids, and he was surely NOT going to pay triple that amount for just one kid, and certainly not to a second woman who left him!

Stephen is brilliant, perhaps the smartest person I have ever known. If he wasn't so damaged from his childhood, he could have been a spectacular adult. His mother was known around the neighborhood as the town drunk; you could find her slumped over a bar all day while his dad was at work and the four siblings were in school. He blamed his father for not taking good enough care of his mom and became what he called "spousified," i.e.: taking it upon himself to try to make her happy, and therefore sober. It didn't work and she died at only 50 years old of an alcohol-related heart attack. Sadly, and ironically, his first wife died an alcohol-related death as well. She was only 49.

For the next several years, Stephen and I battled it out in court. He appealed the child support increase awarded me by the Court and hired a powerful and connected attorney, resolved to punish me for making him a "two-time loser" (his words), and then having the nerve to demand he pay the state minimum in support for our son. I was forced to hire my own $350-an-hour attorney, which would negate any increase the court determined, and Stephen knew that. He and his attorneys filed continuance after continuance, refusing to provide court-ordered discovery documents, and I eventually came to learn why.

By this time, he was working as the CEO of a telecom company with an annual salary of over $200,000, plus yearly bonuses and stock options. What started as a simple hearing was then escalated to the Master's level and ultimately, to Pennsylvania Superior Court, where it was determined that his stock awards should be considered additional income available for child support, a case of first impression[38] and now a PA law.

Stephen's answer to this judgment was to sue me for 50/50 shared custody of Julian, which would give him a 20% decrease in his new child support payments. I could no longer afford to retain an attorney as my financial obligation to her had wiped out any increase I'd received and put me into debt.

I was grateful to have Fabio supporting me during this time. Growing up, his father's job as a Federal Judge in DC made him intimately familiar with the ins and outs of the court system. He filed several documents with the court on my behalf and wrote as many pleadings when I was forced to represent myself.

While the child support hearings were all held in Montgomery County where Stephen resided, the custody hearings were heard in neighboring Chester County, the location of our final marital residence together, and where the original custody order had been filed. This benefitted Stephen, as it made it easier to hide the number of filings, which ultimately totaled 32. He hired what's commonly known as a pettifogger, an unscrupulous hack willing to file lawsuits over sweatpants, Pokémon cards, or even taking 4 minutes

---

[38] "Case of First Impression" • A case of first impression is a case that presents a legal issue that has never been decided by the governing jurisdiction.

to open the door at a custody exchange. Once, when Julian overheard me crying in my room and told his dad, Stephen then sued me for crying. The lawsuits were relentless and I found myself in court at least once a month.

I've since come to realize it was both of my husbands who were having a pissing match in court, with Julian and me as pawns. Prior to the court battle, Stephen and I had been friendly enough to go out to dinner and even attend a few concerts together and Fabio didn't like that one bit.

Their answer to any and all conflict is litigation; neither of them is able to process difficult emotions, so hiding behind attorneys is the only way to go. Fabio egged me on and encouraged me to keep going in court with Stephen, acting as though he was my protector and not the puppeteer he actually was. This was all done to create a wedge between my son's father and me with the hope of isolating me away from family and growing more and more dependent on him.

The stress on me was immeasurable; I couldn't sleep a wink. I would call my mom crying and her unsympathetic response was, "You have Hysterical Personality Disorder, Erin." I thought since she was a psychologist, she knew what was wrong with me and I frantically began researching it online. *That's it!* I said to myself. *That's what's wrong with me. Why has she never told me before? She's a psychologist. I could have been on my way to healing by now.*

I searched and searched and searched and found there's no such thing as Hysterical Personality Disorder; it simply doesn't exist. My mom has never been available to me in times of trouble and she never would be. *Sweep it under the rug. Pretend it's not happening, and what are you doing, Erin, to create this mess?* I've had to unlearn taking responsibility for the actions of others, because *sometimes Erin, other people deserve the blame when bad things happen, like rape or bullying in court.*

Shortly after this period, my mom and I entered therapy together, perhaps the worst decision of my life. I tippy-toed through the first few sessions, not wanting to anger her. From a very young age, I'd learned to table it, shut it down, and not make waves. The therapy was her idea, but it was destined to fail. I hadn't yet fully learned what kind of daughter she wanted me to be and she was never the mother I'd wished for.

I cautiously tried to communicate to her what I needed from her. I wanted her to be able to see me and support me, and not always put the blame on me. I began by telling her I thought she'd done a pretty good job of parenting right up until I was 10 years old, but that I felt she'd checked out to focus on herself when we moved to New Jersey. It was during those pivotal years that she became preoccupied with pursuing a degree in Psychology so she'd be able to support herself and finally leave my dad. My brother and I were still teens and needed her more than ever.

"Oh, so now I'm a bad mom," she blurted out, holding back tears.

The therapist said, "I don't think that's what she's saying, Kit."

"Therapy OVER," she declared, stood up, and marched out of the office for good, leaving the therapist and me sitting there speechless and bewildered. Therapy over, indeed.

All that came of counseling was that I finally had to accept I could never be myself in the presence of my mom. She wasn't capable of handling my roller coaster emotions so I put a permanent lid on it and sought the guidance of friends whenever I was feeling overwhelmed. It seemed to work and our relationship continued to improve year after year until we found a safe spot for both of us to reside.

8.

MOVING IN TOGETHER:
APRIL 2001

In early 2001, Fabio persuaded me to sell my beloved, little rowhouse in Manayunk so we could move in together. We would use the proceeds from the sale to purchase a much larger home for the four of us, closer to where he was living at the time and in his daughter's very desirable school district. I wanted to fulfill my life's dream of having a family, the family I'd never had, hoping to repair the childhood wounds I'd carried inside me for so many years. Ours would be a blended family with two perfect kids (a girl and a boy), a puppy, a kitten, and the proverbial white picket fence. I agreed and sold my home for $100,000, which was used for the down payment on a four-bedroom Colonial fixer-upper with a ton of potential in the peaceful, scenic, and affluent Main Line neighborhood called Mount Misery.

I was 40 years old when we first met, and 41 when we set up house together. That 100,000 dollars represented all the money I'd ever made in my life. Fabio had zero cash to put down; in fact, he had 10 different credit cards with a total of $70,000 worth of debt which he attributed to his first wife who was "too lazy and spoiled" to work. *I can fix this right up,* I thought. *I'll show him how to manage his money. I'm really good with money. He'll never say that about me; I'm a very hard worker.*

Full speed ahead to the perfect family. I had the down payment money, but without his employment income, we would never have qualified for a jumbo mortgage. I told him I wanted us to sign an agreement to protect my investment. An agreement that would give me the first $100,000 of proceeds if we ever split up or sold the house. A portion of that money came from the divorce settlement from my first marriage, and Stephen and I both felt strongly that Julian should be the eventual beneficiary of it.

"You know, I can write that agreement and save you a bunch of money," offered Fabio.

It seemed like a good idea at the time. I had no reason not to trust him… not yet. He's not a lawyer but qualified to "play one on TV." He'd written legal documents for me on many occasions before, during my child support and custody battles with Stephen. He drafted the agreement and we signed it together in front of a notary public. I placed two copies in my Household file, and there they stayed for the next 16 years.

A little bit at a time, I let him take over all the details of our lives. It felt nice for the first time in my life to be able to sit back, relax, and allow someone else to take care of things for me. He handled everything and it was exactly what I thought I'd always wanted.

The house sat on a 2.5-acre wooded lot surrounded by majestic, 100-foot-tall black oak trees, and northern white pines, with flowering mountain laurel bushes scattered among them. There was a lot to do, both inside and out, but we enjoyed home renovation projects and were excited to take on the challenge. I'd learned some skills while fixing up the 250-year-old farmhouse my family had purchased in Jersey, back in 1970, when we first moved out of Manhattan. Fabio apprenticed with the contractors who built the family room addition on his childhood home. He was handy in all sorts of ways.

Together we renovated the entire 3,000-sq.-ft. house from basement to roof. We knocked down walls to create an open floor plan and refinished the floors. Once the footprint was the way we wanted it, he renovated the entire kitchen by himself and all I had to do was choose the appliances, finishes, and paint the walls. It took him over a year but the final result was stunning.

Allow me a quick moment to tell you about "The Great Blender Incident." Fabio loved his peanut butter sandwiches with chocolate milkshakes. One day, while whipping one up in our makeshift kitchen, he neglected to remove the spoon prior to turning on the blender. As we both stood there about one foot apart, we suddenly heard a loud crack, and a thick shard of glass the size of a golf ball was catapulted away from the blender and flew directly between us. Chocolate shake sprayed across the room to the opposite wall and splattered all over the ceiling above us. We laughed nervously together and joked about what "could have" happened and how the headlines would read, but now I wonder if it was the very first sign from the Universe that my future was in imminent danger.

I asked him for a Frank Lloyd Wright–style, stained-glass window above the sink in the kitchen overlooking the backyard straight out to the woods. No problem. He cut right through the back of the house and doubled the size of the window for me, bathing the first floor in a soft wash of blue and yellow light. Next up, he took a reciprocating saw and cut through the exterior brick wall of the house, and widened the front entry to include a door with stained-glass side panels and a transom above. Then he cut another opening in the back of the house adding double-pane French doors leading out to a multi-tiered deck. The deck was one of the few things we'd hired out but the contractor did a shitty job. Rather than make waves with the builder, Fabio just rebuilt the deck himself, making it flush with the edge of the house, just the way I wanted it. I felt like a princess. What couldn't this guy do? *He must really love me.*

"As you wish," was all he ever said to her.

Fabio then renovated all four bathrooms, without any help. He was a master tiler. Everyone who came to the house and saw his work was rightfully impressed and told me how lucky I was to find such a great guy. For the laundry room floor, I chose 12-inch square, Spanish terracotta tiles.

"What color grout do you want, Erin?"

"Gray, please, like the color of concrete."

I left the house to run a few errands but when I returned I saw glossy, pitch-black grout between the tiles.

I didn't want to make him feel bad or criticize him when he'd worked so hard, but the moment I saw it my heart sank, and I quickly brushed past him to cry in the den. *Gray is gray and black is black and they are clearly different colors, but how could I be so mean as to make him redo it? Had he even heard me? Maybe he's colorblind; lots of men are.* I convinced myself I'd be okay with it but Fabio knew I wasn't. Like the hero he was, he rushed straight out to Home Depot and discovered that they sold something called grout colorant. On his hands and knees, he painted the colorant between each and every tile until it was perfect.

He chopped wood for our fireplace, did all the snow blowing in the winter, and raked leaves in the fall. He was like a big bear, my big protective bear. Before we owned a professional 10HP leaf blower he would rake the leaves by hand onto a huge tarp and lug them to the backyard to toss them into the massive quarry we called "our crater" behind the house. Nothing could stop him, and it was totally sexy. The married ladies around the Mountain were all jealous of me. My husband was fit and strong, helpful and hot, and theirs were fat and balding, sitting on the couch watching sports with a beer in hand all weekend, while we were making love on our leaf-free front lawn.

When the next-door neighbor accidentally broke our leaf blower and the repair shop declared it unfixable, he went online and ordered a new motor. When that didn't work, he wasn't going to give up and bought a special spacer tool that fixed it permanently. From time to time, our basement would flood, and one time he rigged a tiny pump from a fish tank with some leftover catheter tubing from a bout with a kidney stone. He then siphoned it and fed it directly into the air conditioner condenser pan, clearing the basement of a foot of water in just two days. Living on Mount Misery also meant regular power outages during ice storms and my MacGyver was so smart and so clever, he figured out how to hook up my Toyota Prius battery to power the fridge and the TV, sometimes for as long as five days.

Even in the kitchen, he handled all the dirty stuff I didn't want to – touching the raw chicken and deveining the shrimp. I loved going to the grocery store with him to pick out fresh food for dinner. He was a master of the outdoor grill, and all I had to do were the side dishes and the clean-up. He changed the oil in our cars. *How did I get so lucky to find such a talented and helpful partner?*

I thought I'd met my soulmate. For the first time in my life, I finally felt seen, safe, and cared for.

This is true love. You think this happens every day?

We carried matching monogrammed key rings for 20 years, best-friend broken heart pins attached to our car visors. Once while shopping with Fabio and my mom in

Lambertville, I gushed over a turquoise choker necklace that cost over $100. I really wanted it but didn't want to spend that kind of money so I walked away from it and out of the shop. The next thing I knew, Fabio said he needed to find a bathroom but had actually gone back to the store and came back to surprise me with the necklace I loved. He hand-sewed Julian's little stuffed bunny after the dog destroyed it and ripped all of the stuffing out. *What had I done to deserve this amazing man?*

But over time, little nuggets of arrogance began to surface. Sure, he was helpful, but try as I may, I couldn't feel emotionally connected to him. I began to wonder if he was doing all these home projects to avoid spending quality time with the family. He would mutter things like, "It's tough being in the top 2%, surrounded by the lower 98." I thought he was joking. He had a deadpan humor and spoke without much inflection in his voice.

While grocery shopping, he was the only one allowed to push the cart, but whenever we came upon someone inadvertently parked in the middle of the aisle, he would just stand there like a totem pole with a nasty look on his face, waiting for the other shopper to feel his stare-down and turn around to see how "thoughtless" they were for blocking his path. I said to him, "Why don't you just say, 'excuse me?'" He didn't want to be "rude," just hostile. At the check-out line, he refused to help bag groceries even if the line behind us was 20 people deep.

"My dad told me that if I went to college, I'd never have to bag groceries," he snickered.

Alternately, if he was at the back of the line, he'd be complaining about anyone that had purchased "too many" groceries or was writing a check, always grumbling under his breath, while trashing others.

I said to him, "I don't like myself when I'm with you. The only way I can connect with you is to be negative, and to trash other people." He didn't care. He didn't like other people.

I began to wonder if he even loved me so I asked him, "Why do you love me?"

"What, why would you ask me that?"

I tried to phrase it another way hoping he would understand my words. "What about me do you love?"

"I don't know, I just do."

I could tell he didn't have an answer. He didn't know either.

Suddenly, the man who once loved my vegetarian lasagna only ate five foods. When dining out and asked if he would like soup or salad, he would simply state, "I'm not a salad guy." He wasn't a soup guy either, and not really a vegetable guy. All he would eat was plain chicken or meat and how he ordered it at a restaurant was by telling the server, "I'll have the chicken sandwich, just chicken and bread." If the waitress asked him "Would you like lettuce and tomato on that?" he strongly repeated, "Just chicken and bread."

"How about mayo?"

Angrily now, between his teeth, "CHICKEN AND BREAD." When the server left the table, he would complain to me about how stupid they were. The same applied to burgers – no condiments, no nothing – just burger and bread. At home, he made himself plain steaks, peanut butter without jelly, or plain pizza made from scratch – five nights a week. "Toppings are for sissies, no one likes toppings!" No eggs for breakfast, only bread products, like toast, cereal, bagels, or pancakes. Pasta was out too. He may have two crowns of broccoli once or twice per week, but only with "broccoli stuff," a mixture of breadcrumbs and butter poured over the top.

Whenever he chewed, food would fall out of his mouth. It was gross, so I would avert my eyes. He seemed unaware of his surroundings and I began to feel a sense of uneasiness when around him. In the morning, he would wake up before me and head down to the kitchen to start the coffee before returning upstairs to our home office for his telecommuting job at R.O.U.S Industries. When I went downstairs for my cup of coffee, I would step on coffee grounds all over the floor tiles and find a trail of sugar on the counter. *I'm the only one who cares,* reminding yours truly of Stephen's "helpful" words and resigned myself to clean up after him. *This is not worth mentioning, Erin.*

Because he woke up before me, he was the one to feed the dog. In the winter months, I would come downstairs to find he'd left the side door wide open with snow and cold air blowing in through the laundry room. It was freezing, but Fabio was oblivious; he'd already gone upstairs to work.

"Hey honey, can you close the door behind you when you feed the dog?"

"What? The cat was underfoot, I got distracted, I forgot…"

"Well, you may need to push it closed behind you; it doesn't always close by itself." No follow-up response, only an eye roll. This happened every single day; I would ask him to please close the door and he would harrumph at me, blaming it on the cat. I remembered Stephen didn't like being told what to do and rather than "nag" him, asked that I make a list of "honey-do" chores and tape it to the pantry door. A year later Stephen hadn't checked off a single item but maybe this would work for Fabio. I placed a reminder note next to the back door and every day he "forgot" to close it I would make a little hashtag mark. Ninety marks later I took it down.

I kept trying to convince myself he was just different, and that maybe my expectations of him were unreasonable. He was so sweet and he made me laugh, he was talented and helpful. I was lucky, right? That's what all the neighbor ladies told me.

He could be funny and sarcastic with a dry wit, just like his idol, Keith Richards. Keith never says much but his well-placed words are always insightful, impactful, and quite clever. "Timing is everything," Fabio would say. He would try and slip a punchline into a conversation but go immediately silent if the timing wasn't just perfect. Some of his one-liners had me rolling in stitches every time he would repeat them. The day after a snowfall he would point out the SNIRT (a combination of snow and dirt). Funny, right? I thought so too. The albino squirrel that lived on Mount Misery was a squirrel dentist, a tennis pro, or wearing a bridal gown off to get married.

He looked up to people who used very few words; they were the "cool guys," the ones he wanted to emulate. Kwai Chang Caine[39] of *Kung Fu* fame was a childhood idol, as well as Mr. Spock from *Star Trek*. I reminded myself again, *he's the strong, silent type. Be good with it Erin, he loves you. Look at everything he's done for you.*

One day I came home from the salon and walked into the kitchen to show Fabio my new "do." I stepped into the room, stood completely still, grinning ear to ear at him. He gave me a puzzled look and inquired, "Did you get your hair done?" I proceeded to bend over to show him the four subtle pink stripes that were carefully hidden in the underside of my hair. They weren't visible while I was standing up, only if I turned my head to the side quickly, or flipped it over. I hung there for a minute, with my head upside down, waiting to hear his hopefully positive reaction. Long pause. Eventually, I heard him speak sharply, "Now why would you go and do a thing like that?" I

---

[39] "Kwai Chang Caine" • Lead character in the popular TV series *Kung Fu*, which aired in the U.S. from 1972–1975.

felt a sting in my gut, immediately righted myself, and looked at him quizzically. Then came the final nail in the coffin. "At your age?" I felt stupid and ashamed, wondering if he was right and if other people would think I was pathetic, trying to look younger than I was.

I couldn't always tell if he was kidding, because some of his statements seemed passive-aggressive,[40] but my cognitive dissonance skills overrode my feelings again and again, and I would tell myself, *he didn't mean it.*

I started noticing something else I didn't like about him; he was forever playing the victim card. His first wife, Laura, had forced him to sell his waterfront property in St. Pete because she wanted to live closer to her mom in New Jersey. It was her fault he had to give up his dream of a career in filmmaking and live in the cold weather. She lied to him too, saying she enjoyed renovating houses but he ended up doing all the work, while she lay in bed reading all day. She was a terrible mother; he had to play the role of both Mom and Dad to their daughter. He referred to her as "Psycho Bitch" and called her that regularly in front of Layla. I asked him not to, for Layla's sake, but he just wouldn't stop.

My charming prince was gone and in his place stood a mopey, sad-sack, just like Eeyore... all the red lights he encountered contained what he called a "Fabio Detector," as if every traffic light saw him coming and

---

[40] "Passive-Aggressive" • A way of expressing negative feelings, such as anger or annoyance, indirectly instead of directly.

turned red just before he got there. Everyone drives slowly in front of him too, and that's why he's always late for everything. As an empathic person, I wanted to try and help him turn his attitude around, to see the good in people, the beauty in the world.

I once asked him for a massage and what he had to offer was truly pathetic. He made no effort whatsoever – this from a guy who kneads dough and makes himself a personal pizza five days a week. When I asked if he could apply a bit more pressure he gave up instantly, jumped up, and said, "I'm no good at this." It was his way of getting out of ever giving me a massage again, and it worked; I never asked again. It reminded me of Stephen, who did the same shitty job whenever I would ask him to help out with the household chores or tackle an item on the "honey-do" list.

"I worked all week!"

His internal anxiety was through the roof; I just couldn't understand why. Always picking at his hands and feet until they bled; he kept Band-Aid in business, all by himself! I would gently pass my hand between his two hands to try and discourage him but three seconds later, he was right back at it.

Everything he did, he did very slowly. Growing up in New York City made me just the opposite; I'm like Speedy Gonzales. "Opposites attract," he would say, but I would spend most of my weekends waiting on him to finish working, to be available to spend just a little bit of time doing something fun with me.

I never understood why his "process" took forever. He would tell me he was just being thorough, unlike the others who rushed into things and made mistakes. Yet another opportunity to trash folks. Of course, he made mistakes too; it just took him longer. He would stare at the wall and make multiple trips to Home Depot before even getting started.

Working at a snail's pace, every home project took a year or two to complete. Granted, he was working a full-time job during this period, he did save us a lot of money, and the project was always spectacular when finished, but it felt like he was moving slowly on purpose, using the burden of home renovation as an excuse to avoid interacting with the family. All I wanted to do was go for a bike ride or take a walk with him, but the hours would pass by, with me wasting time on Facebook and him making fun of me for it until it was time to make dinner. I felt rejected but wouldn't allow myself to dwell on it.

We began to fight pretty regularly, yelling back and forth at each other in the den. I was trying to reach him, to get him to hear me, to consider my needs too, but all he would do is scream back louder, "What are you, a lawyer?" *No, Fabio, that's you.* After every fight, he would threaten to leave me, and one by one, take all of Layla's pictures off the wall. I would just stand there, not moving, saying nothing. What a drama queen he was! I told myself he was afraid of confrontation, but his avoidance and lack of response to my concerns created even more of it.

It was all so confusing. He was so awesome, so talented and helpful, yet so distant and moody. Our conversations went in circles; I never felt he understood what I was saying so I would repeat myself to him in different ways.

Me: Why do you talk to me like I'm stupid?

Him: I don't think you're stupid.

Me: I didn't say that. I don't care what you think of my intelligence. Why do you speak to me as though I were stupid?

Him: I DON'T think you're stupid.

Me: I don't care if you think I'm stupid or smart. Why do you talk down to me?

Him: I don't.

Me: That's not for you to determine. I'm asking, why are you so dismissive?

Him: I'm not. Why do you keep saying that?

And round and round we go again…

Me: You don't understand anything I say!

Him: I understand EVERYTHING you say.

I wondered if it was intentional but quickly dismissed that notion and convinced myself that he wasn't paying attention, or was simply trying to avoid conflict. I never thought he was gaming me.

9.

I'M AFRAID OF
WHAT I MIGHT DO TO YOU!:
FALL 2001

I don't even remember what this fight was about but I will never forget the first time witnessing the transformation of my future husband into a werewolf. I was standing outside the kitchen and he was three steps down in the den. We were arguing, probably about his daughter Layla, when I suddenly became aware that he was physically shaking, hard, as if he were about to have a seizure.

I froze solid in the moment. All of a sudden, his eyes rolled back into their sockets, fists clenched at his sides, still shaking with eyes glaring and glowing black; he screamed at me in a bone-chilling voice, "I'm afraid of what I might DO to you!" Then he ran outside into the backyard and disappeared to who knows where for several hours. When he finally returned, he walked right past me and up the stairs to bed without saying a single word. I always felt if I had pressured him in that dissociative moment, he might have killed me with a kitchen knife, so I played it cool and stayed out of his way for the next several days.

10.
ISOLATION/INSTILLING FEAR AND DEPENDENCE: 2001–2005

Mount Misery is an upscale, secluded community, nestled in the woods adjacent to Valley Forge National Historical Park. It was only five minutes from the largest mall in America at the time, but you would never know it from the beautiful, stately mansions, each one positioned on 2.5 acres of pristine, wooded property. No cars in the street, only nature noises could be heard… wind in the trees, birds singing, deer and wild critters rustling around in the woods. This is where the rich folks live; we were only pretending to fit in.

It was a very social community with plenty of annual events. If they didn't have parties, they would never see each other for the privacy of each property. Ironically, when we first moved in, I found out that one of my former interns from WMMR was living directly across the street and was a frequent neighborhood party host. I wanted to get to know my new neighbors and my old intern Caryn's parties were the best place to accomplish that, but living with someone as socially awkward as Fabio, it was always a balance between my need to socialize and his need to skedaddle from the party as quickly as possible.

At one of these parties, we were all downstairs in their "party room," complete with a fully-stocked bar and professional bartender. I was milling about the crowd, making new friends, when I noticed Fabio standing like a totem pole on the staircase landing, arms folded, surveying the crowd but talking to no one. I went over to ask why he wasn't trying to meet people and he replied, "I have to stand watch in case someone here tries to hurt you." I said, "What? On Mount Misery?" He said, "You never know…" and that planted the first seed of doubt for my own safety at home.

For the next 15 years, we left every party in the middle, sneaking out. Fabio assured me no one noticed. I chalked it up to his social anxiety, so I didn't pressure him to stay. Although I'm sure people DID see us leaving and formed a negative opinion of me since Fabio was so stealth at remaining invisible in social situations and I was the more talkative one.

When we walked the dog around the neighborhood he would always stay three steps behind me, which I found extremely frustrating. "Can you walk next to me so I don't have to turn around to talk to you?"

"But if I walk behind you, I can see someone approaching to attack you before they reach you and block them from behind."

Huh? On Mount Misery there are attackers?

He even went so far as to build me a "safe room" tucked into one of the attic eaves off our master bedroom. It locked from the inside and came complete with instructions and a burner phone to call the police if my first husband ever came to the house to try and kill me. Needless to say, I never felt safe in the world without him to "protect" me, and that's the way he wanted it.

He did all this to instill fear and a dependency on him to "protect" me from harm that may come from outside the marriage when in truth it was to deflect from the fact that it was already coming from within.

11.

THE RAPE FANTASY MYTH: 2002

I never realized that absolutely everything boiled down to sex with Fabio, and what I mean by that is his narcissistic injury has to do with his "size." Had I known the depth of his pain and insecurity, I would have tread more lightly in this area. Sex was always a thing, and by a thing, I mean a problem. His inability to initiate sex was due to his fear of rejection and he COULDN'T be rejected, EVER; he even said so. He said the reason he was not good at initiating was because when he was younger, girls threw themselves at him so he never even had to try. I later found this to be the exact opposite of the truth.

So, it became my job to initiate sex each and every time and over the years and years of passive-aggressive comments and emotional abuse, I began to pull away from him, and it became less and less often. He asked me to take male hormones, anything that would get him more sex. It wasn't that he wasn't attractive to me, or that I didn't want or enjoy sex, it was that he was abusive. When I pointed out that most people complain they get less sex after they got married, he would bark, "I don't CARE about other people!" Little did I know how true that statement was.

I tried to make it easier for him by promising I'd never reject him if he would approach me on Sunday mornings. I even gave him a simple phrase to try, "Are you up for some naked time?"

He always seemed anxious and preoccupied during sex, like he wasn't even present. He never made a sound in bed and when I asked why, his response was always, "So I can last longer," but 'longer' with Fabio was only six minutes. I know that because I watched the bedroom clock on the nightstand, and counted down. I guessed by his proclamation that if he did express any enjoyment out loud, sex may only last two minutes; I'll never know.

Early in our relationship, during "The Act," I once asked Fabio if he could go a little harder, a bit faster, not realizing his deep fear of "falling out" and not being able to do what I'd requested. He immediately jumped off me and out of bed, screaming at me in a terrifying rage, "All women want to be raped, all women have a rape fantasy." I was petrified, naked, lying there frozen yet somehow, was able to respond with, "Even your daughter, even your mother?"

"You are a fucking whore," and then he stormed out of the room. Lovely, right? That's not going to get you more sex, buddy. Had I realized the depth of his emotional damage I'd have left him a long time ago but I kept trying to help him learn to be happy and trust others, and to make the marriage work.

12.

PREGNANT WOMEN DON'T CLEAN THE CAT PAN: 2003

In the early '00s, I was managing a NYC-based power pop band called The Rosenbergs. Lead singer and songwriter David Fagin, Evan, Mahoney, and Zeckle were all staying at our house for a week to record with Eric Bazilian, a close friend, local celebrity rock star, and record producer. Eric was a founding member of the Philadelphia band The Hooters, and GRAMMY-nominated composer of Joan Osborne's Top Five hit, "One of Us."

It was around 10 a.m. when I gathered the boys to head over to the studio for the day. As we were leaving, I realized I'd forgotten to do something so I called up to Fabio from the bottom of the stairs, "Hey Fabio, can you clean the cat pan? I didn't get a chance to." When I returned from dropping the band at the studio, Fabio asked me, "Are you pregnant?" I said, "WHAT?" He repeated, "Are you pregnant?" I replied, "No, what would give you that idea?" He said, "You asked me to clean the cat pan. Pregnant women shouldn't clean cat pans." I reassured him that I just didn't have the time before I had to drive to the studio.

Over the years, his story changed with my words evolving to match his abandonment fears.

From: Can you clean the cat pan? I didn't get a chance to.

To: Can you clean the cat pan, because I am pregnant?

To: Can you clean the cat pan? I'm pregnant and pregnant women shouldn't clean the cat pan.

To: Can you clean the cat pan? I am pregnant by David Fagin, and pregnant women shouldn't clean the cat pan.

Eric was the first of my male friends that Fabio made clear he thought was "not my friend." Eric and I share a birthday and celebrated together for almost 20 years before I met Fabio, but Eric was extremely good-looking, and that made him a threat. Toward the end of The Rosenbergs' recording session, Fabio threw a major wrench into that relationship, one that was never fully repaired.

Eric and I agreed to do this recording project on a handshake, but once the demos started to come out well, he changed his mind and decided we needed a contract. Without advance notification, I received a call from his attorney and that's all Fabio needed to start the poisoning process with my friend.

"See? He's out for himself. He doesn't care about you. He didn't even tell you himself, he had a lawyer do it."

Fabio had a way of telling the truth, but spinning it so that it sounded completely negative and paranoid, and I was easily influenced by him at that time. I wanted to believe he was on my side, that he was looking out for me, but he had ulterior motives and that was to separate me from my friends, family, and support system and he started with my better-looking male friends. Eric was the first to go; David Fagin would be next.

13.

IN AND OUT OF THERAPY/
THE LAYLA YEARS

Layla's initial reaction to me had been surprising and deeply upsetting. I've always been great with kids and my other step-kids took to me immediately. Fabio thought the best way to introduce her to the idea of a new family was to tread lightly and gingerly while wearing his guilt about bringing a new woman into her life like a cloak.

He concocted a backhanded way of introducing us by trying to orchestrate a run-in at the grocery store where we would pretend to be casual acquaintances and I would ask him to feed my cats while I was away for the weekend. Layla loved animals so by bringing her along to help out, our relationship could develop gradually. I thought he was overthinking it. I know how to act around kids, but since it was his kid, I deferred to him. That plan was foiled the day she unexpectedly burst into his condo, took one look at me and screamed, "make her go away!" and ran upstairs crying. The best-laid plans of mice and men... and we were off to a rocky start.

The scheme he devised to inform her we were all moving in together was even worse. We'd been working with a realtor for months but he avoided even mentioning it to her. Once we purchased the home in Valley Forge there was no turning back so he brought her to see the house, and asked if she liked it, and would she like to live in it? Layla replied, "No." Best-laid plans again, Fabio.

Layla is supremely intuitive and knew she was being manipulated. She's no dummy and could tell that he was lying and that her feelings about it had not even been considered. She shouldn't have had the power to prevent it but should have been included in the discussion long before she ever was. I was furious with him. If he'd involved her in the process from the very beginning, the outcome could have been so much better. I felt like I was being portrayed as a punishment for her.

He didn't seem to understand what it took to be a good father. *No worries, Erin, you can fix this too.*

I pointed out the mistakes he was making with her, and he would explain that the reason he indulged her and could never say no was because his dad died when they were at odds with each other and he'd lived a "life of guilt and regret" as a result of it. I would plead with him to listen to me. "Fabio, you can't live your life in fear of dying while at odds with your daughter. She needs boundaries to feel safe in the world," but his need for her to be dependent on him trumped both my needs and hers.

Every Saturday morning, Layla would ultimately roll out of bed around 10 a.m., long after the rest of us were up, come down the stairs, and be greeted by the following:

Fabio: "Good morning, Pookie! Can I get you something to eat? How about pancakes? Or would you rather have crepes and jam? Maybe yogurt and fruit? I could always make you some eggs. Would you like scrambled or fried? We have cereal. What about grits, or biscuits with clotted cream? How does a chocolate muffin sound? Or would you rather have blueberry?"

Layla would cock her cute little curly head and say, "Daddy, do we have any jelly donuts?"

Fabio: "No honey, but no problem. I'll run out to the store and get you some."

I never realized at the time that spoiling Layla satisfied two important needs for him – one, he could always be the favorite parent, thereby triangulating Layla against her mother; and two, after his divorce and before I arrived on the scene, Layla had been an unconditionally loving source of narcissistic supply and he wasn't willing to risk losing her hero-worship of him.

"Fabio, you're ruining her chances of ever having a good relationship when she grows up. Who's going to offer her a list of menu options for breakfast?" He scoffed at me, then rolled his eyes. What did I know about parenting? Clearly nothing.

The consequence of being his main source of supply for the past three years rendered her unable to make a decision for herself. She would spend 20 minutes deciding on a snack. If two of her friends asked her to get together on the same day she'd be paralyzed with anxiety.

Layla: "But if I go sledding and it's too cold I'll wish I'd gone to the movies with Mia, and if I go to the movies and it's a nice day I'll wish I had gone sledding. Daddy, what should I do?"

He took her to the same hotel he and I had visited the year before in Oahu, the one he'd taken me to when I earned my Open Water Diver certification on the North Shore. Right from the very beginning, he set us up in competition with each other again and again. When he gave me a fancy, white French Riviera-style beach chair as a present, she complained, so he bought a sewing machine and promised to make her a "better" homemade chair.

Things got weirder and weirder once we moved in together. He and Laura had an odd custody arrangement, whereby Layla would spend two days with Mom, then two with Dad with the weekends alternating between the two. He said it was because she hated her mom and couldn't stand more than two days at a time with her. He had me convinced that if he moved too quickly her mom would poison her against us by telling her, "Your dad abandoned me and he will leave you too!"

On the nights she was with us, he would spend the hour before bedtime reading to her while lying next to her in her waterbed. He called it Daddy-Daughter Alone Time and told me that she was the one who'd requested it but whenever I tried to open the door, it was locked from the inside. *Don't let that bother you, Erin. It is weird, but who are you to judge others' parenting?*

I would come downstairs on school days to find her sitting in his lap while he braided her hair, which continued until she was 14 years old. They watched TV together in the den, spooning on the couch like lovers or worse yet, with her lying flat on his stomach. It gave me a bad feeling in my gut, but I chose to ignore it.

At times, I would come home to find them sitting on either end of the couch in the den, staring at opposite walls without talking, without any TV or music playing. It was a really awkward vibe.

"Layla and I don't need to talk to feel close to each other," he snapped, but much later, when I reconnected with her as an adult and reminded her of it, her eyes bulged out and she said, "Yeah, that WAS weird!"

If I ever said anything about his parenting he would flip out and start a fight with me, behaving like a toddler, ripping all her pictures off the walls and sulking, saying that I clearly hated her and if it would make me happy, he would remove all traces of her.

I suggested we try family counseling. I thought maybe with the help of a therapist I could teach him how to set appropriate boundaries with his daughter, thereby saving her and little me all over again. Layla dug in her heels and barely participated in the sessions. She would sit and look at the floor while he spoke as little as possible, leaving me to tell the story, looking like the complainer, the one with the problem. I was only trying to help them develop a healthy father-daughter relationship. The counselor would implore him, "Fabio, she shouldn't want it. At this age, she should be the one pushing back, and you should respect that." He was deaf, dumb, and blind to anyone's input. Multiple counselors later, I gave up and she moved to her mom's house for the rest of high school.

Fabio couldn't handle it; it was my fault that she left. He didn't think she would last a week with her mom and frequently blamed me for her moving out. Her master-suite bedroom was kept as a shrine for the next two years while Julian stayed in the tiny room across the hall. We even kept her stinky guinea pigs because Laura wouldn't allow them at her place. Laura had actual rules.

The summer before she was to enter Georgetown University, and after many fights with her mother, she decided to give us another try. I was ready for a fresh start too and welcomed her home with open arms. The only problem was that they'd neglected to tell Laura she was moving out and emptied all her possessions into a truck while her mother was away at work. When I came home that evening and stepped into the house, I heard someone screaming on our answering machine. I walked into the kitchen and heard Laura's voice.

"How dare you! That's my furniture, those things belong to me. I'm calling the police."

I called upstairs, "Layla, are you okay?" She meekly replied, "Yes, I'm sorry, she's *craaaazy*."

That summer between high school and college was a good one for Layla and me. We attended yoga classes together and finally formed a little bond of our own. I knew she'd only be with us a couple of months and was too old now for Fabio to be locking her in the bedroom for "Daddy-Daughter Alone Time." She had lots of really nice friends and was a very good friend herself. Wicked-smart and dedicated to her studies, she was preparing to enter Georgetown University on a partial scholarship majoring in Criminal Justice.

She stayed with us each summer for the next three years, and when graduation time rolled around, Fabio wanted to pay off one of her education loans as a gift. The loan was for a little over $8,000. I suggested we give her 10 grand in cash, which she could use for rent or to buy a car while looking for a government job in DC. He was surprised by the generosity of my offer but I had an ulterior motive. I wanted to ensure she stayed in DC so her dad wouldn't treat her like a child anymore. She was a capable adult now but his doting made her unsure of herself at times.

The very next weekend, I came home from work to find Layla in the upstairs bedroom and moved back in with us. I asked Fabio why she was there and why hadn't he told me she was moving home. I thought we had an understanding. He stonewalled me, refusing to respond. I felt duped and my heart sank once again. He was back to his old tricks and I could feel my resentment for him growing. *He never listens to me! What do I have to do to be heard around here? Mom, tap tap tap tap tap.*

I asked him if we could all sit down together and talk it over, a family meeting of sorts, and he agreed. That Sunday evening the three of us gathered at the dining table and I asked Layla why she felt the need to move home. She seemed really nervous, like maybe she wasn't aware that we expected her to stay in her DC apartment while looking for a job.

"We gave you $10,000 to use for rent, Layla, why did you come home?"

She replied, her voice trembling, "Well, that would only last five months!"

She sounded like a true brat and continued, "All of my other friends moved home after school. They all got money and cars!"

Sigh, this had to stop. $10,000 is a lot of money and I wanted her to have faith in herself so she could land the dream job she wanted and protect her from Fabio's clutches. I felt powerless in that moment and realized that Fabio wasn't saying a single word. He was triangulating in silence, watching the two of us go at each other, until… "Daddy, GET ME OUT OF HERE!" They both stood up, leaving me at the table alone, packed her bags, and left. I felt like a monster.

The next few weeks were a whirlwind for Layla. She stayed with a friend for a while and then used some of the money we gave her to buy a car and drove to Florida into the arms of her loving grandmother Evelyn (aka GiGi). She must have felt discarded, so unwanted, but that was never my intention. I wanted her to launch, to fly, and not be dependent on her dad any longer.

Once she arrived in Florida and told GiGi what happened, I became the family pariah.

"Divorce her, and kick her to the curb. She abused my granddaughter," Evelyn told Fabio. At least that's what he told me she'd said. She later told me that she never said that, but I was now a Venditti outsider, and Evelyn and I would never feel comfortable together again.

In the end, Layla turned out okay. In fact, she's better than okay. I like to think I had a little something to do with it. I just wish everything had been different and that she and I were allowed to develop a natural relationship together. Today she is a Federal Officer, having graduated from the extremely challenging FLETC[41] program after two tries. Just like me, Layla is not a quitter! Most people would give up on their dreams long before Layla would.

---

[41] "FLETC" • Federal Law Enforcement Training Centers

14.

SECOND MARRIAGE: JANUARY AND JUNE 2004

We lived together as "Tenants in Common" for almost three years after purchasing the Valley Forge house. At Julian's Back-to-School nights the teacher would ask him, "Are you Julian's father?" Fabio would reply, "I live wit' dem," using a voice that made him sound like Frankenstein. But after suffering five years of triangulation with Layla I suggested that maybe if we got married she might feel more secure that he wasn't going to abandon her and he agreed. How romantic!

He never proposed. Well, maybe sort of when we were first dating and I found myself between jobs without health insurance, he'd given me a sideways glance. How romantic!

There was no engagement ring and I had to pick out my own wedding band from a site on the Internet. How romantic!

He never proposed to Laura either. Who knows why; maybe that way he couldn't be held responsible for his future actions.

There is a unique form of marriage in Pennsylvania where you don't need an officiant present for the union to be completely legal and binding. In the Quaker tradition, a couple can obtain a self-uniting marriage license as long as they have two witnesses to sign for them. You could actually go to the mall and ask a couple of complete strangers if you wanted to. Fabio researched all of this, as he did with everything, and we drove to the Chester County Courthouse in West Chester, where for a mere $100, we received our self-uniting marriage license. Three days later we crossed the street to Caryn's house and she and her husband witnessed our union. We all then had bagels and juice and Fabio and I walked back across the street as husband and wife. It was January 1st, 2004, and the start of a new tax year. How romantic!

We kept our legal marriage a secret from friends and family and made our neighbors vow to keep it a secret too. Our "real" *Princess Bride*–themed wedding would take place in June at a historical Bucks County Bed & Breakfast called Holly Hedge Estates.

Mawidge… mawidge is what bwings us togevver today…

The June wedding was an elegant and intimate affair with only 35 guests in attendance, made up of my closest friends and our immediate families. We wrote our own vows derived from our favorite movie, and Fabio's father's brother, Uncle Jeff, "officiated" the ceremony. I wore a bright pink and orange Roberto Cavalli evening gown and gold-leaf Prada sandals. He wore a black, long-tailed suit, not a tux, with a casual white shirt and no tie, black suede Birkenstocks on his feet. Fabio was always going barefoot and the Birks were a formal expression of that.

I asked Layla to be my Maid of Honor, hoping it would create a bond between us and help her feel included in the ceremony as an actual member of our family. She was so nervous and uncomfortable; she completely ignored me all day. As Julian and I emerged to walk down the aisle together arm in arm, I had to walk completely around his Aunt Mary, who was crouched right in the middle of the aisle, taking photos.

I took care of all the wedding details and asked Fabio to plan our honeymoon and asked that it be a surprise for me. The first leg of his honeymoon master plan had us up at 3 a.m. the day after the wedding, to take a 6 a.m. flight to Florida to swim with dolphins. It's something I'd always wanted to do but somehow, while in the pool I came in contact with some evil fire coral. Within 30 minutes of getting out of the pool I felt a strong, burning sensation and stinging pain on my right forearm. Later that evening a dark red, bumpy rash with vesicles filled with pus appeared, and my arm began itching like crazy. I don't know why but something bad always happened to me while traveling with Fabio. I thought I was cursed, but now I know it was him. The Universe was trying to warn me.

The second leg of our honeymoon began with a 5 a.m. flight to Puerto Rico and then off to our final destination, Saint Lucia. Once we landed on the island, we discovered that the helicopter pilot Fabio hired to pick us up and take us to the resort not only wasn't there but couldn't be reached by phone either. We hailed a cab that drove us for two hours on a winding, mountain road through the jungle to the Jalousie Hilton resort on the opposite side of the island. Nestled between Saint Lucia's landmark Pitons,[42] with a private villa at the top of the hill and our very own dunking pool, we settled in for a week in paradise. Every day, once we'd left the room, the maid staff carefully placed tropical wildflowers in patterns of hearts on the crisp white linens.

The diving was exceptional, the coral the most colorful I'd ever seen. I did my first night dive there and witnessed electric eels, transparent fish, and jellyfish, swirling with neon colors. It was terrifying to dive at night, not knowing up from down in the dark waters, but thrilling, and an experience I'll never forget.

We returned from our romantic honeymoon to a voicemail message from my mom saying, "Call me." I immediately dialed her number.

"Your dad died."

"Oh my God, when?"

"On your wedding day. I didn't want to spoil your honeymoon."

---

[42] "Pitons" • A pair of large, volcanic spires on either side of Saint Lucia's Jalousie Bay.

Another sign.

I loved cooking for my new husband. After he finished his work day, we'd head off to Wegmans market to pick out the two very best swordfish steaks. I would loop my arm in his and look up at him with love in my eyes. He never returned that look, but I was determined to show him that I loved him and I guess I was used to not feeling that love coming back at me, but I still kept on trying. *He's showing you love in the form of home projects, Erin. People are different and they don't express love the same way you do. He's a "cool guy," remember? You're just too needy.*

I made him thousands of chicken dinners. Chicken was always a safe bet and parmigiana was his favorite; another was chicken with pesto and toasted pine nuts. I was opening him up to new things like seafood, sauces, different spices, and new ingredients. *He WAS growing, expanding his palate, and it was all because of me! His other women weren't able to do that. He must trust me more than he did them.*

I was proud of myself, to be able to do that for him. His cholesterol was through the roof and I was determined to get it under control so we could live a long, happy, healthy life together. We had a Costco membership and spent hours roaming the wide aisles stocking our pantry and basement fridge with all kinds of mouthwatering delicacies and household necessities. There was plenty of room in the house to store things; he'd hand-built storage shelves in our full basement and added an access door to the massive attic. Whenever we left Costco he rode the shopping cart down the slope in the parking lot, just like a little boy. So sweet! I loved having a family for the first time in my life. It made me happy to cook him dinners while he worked hard on our house and at his job. He would always smile and thank me for cooking.

Fabio took over the kitchen for all the major holidays so I could enjoy spending time with my family. He wasn't much of a conversationalist, and who can get a word in with us Rileys anyway? I would prep the sides before our guests arrived and he remained in the kitchen once they did, basting the turkey, making the stuffing, boiling and mashing the potatoes. The cheesecake he made every Christmas was the best New York–style cheesecake the world has ever known, and we all looked forward to it each year.

We were a great team, with complementary skills. I was the more social, outgoing, and creative one, and he was smart, talented, and the hardest worker I'd ever known. At times I truly felt the domestic bliss I'd always dreamed of.

Like clockwork every month, he would drive to the store to purchase a lottery ticket using our birthdays for the numbers… his, mine, Layla's, and Julian's. The Powerball changed each year to match the number of years we'd been together. He regularly checked unclaimed freight sites for money that might be due to him in hopes of finding a recently-deceased rich relative who'd left him a cool million or two. We had big dreams for our future together, and we would need a lot of money to realize them all.

Every night after dinner we'd settle in to watch TV in the den. In the winter I would build a fire and since he was in charge of the many remotes that controlled the intricate media system he'd installed, he would look for something we could both enjoy together. He frequently deferred to me and my tastes, indulging me by watching girly shows like *Desperate Housewives* or even *Project Runway*; what other guy would do that?

I've always preferred my men to be on the softer side. I could never relate to hyper-manly men – you know, the kind of guys that hoot and holler, beer in hand while punching each other in the arm. I like 'em looking like men but more cerebral, more artistic, and cultured. Fabio fit that bill perfectly. He wore moccasins with a puka-shell shark tooth necklace and it was very sexy. TV time gave the term "sexy" a new meaning – sitting on the leather couch, wearing my blue denim robe wide open, his junk hanging out all the time. *He's comfortable in our home. That's a good thing, right?*

The only sport he watched on TV was the annual Triple Crown and that was the only time I would see him cry; it was so sweet. If ever a horse or jockey suffered an injury or had a heart-wrenching backstory he would weep quietly to himself on the couch with genuine tears rolling down his cheeks. I wished he would share more of that vulnerability with me. I knew it was in there; I just couldn't seem to access it. Occasionally he would utter an uncomfortable sound and I would ask "Honey, are you okay?" "Fine," was all he ever said. I felt shut out.

He would casually mention something that had happened weeks before.

"Why didn't you tell me that?"

"You didn't ask."

"Huh? Am I supposed to run through a list of things that might possibly have happened until I guess correctly? Why don't you want to share your life experiences with me? Why do you need to hide everything?"

Sitting next to him in the office, "Hey, can I ask you a question?"

"You just did."

I would sigh in frustration.

"Can I ask you another question?"

"You just did."

Ugh, the pain of trying to connect with him. Angrily now, "Fabio, can I ask you three questions in a row?"

"Oh, okay, admit it though, that's funny, right?"

No, Fabio, not funny. Not the 400th time.

My childhood triggers are not feeling seen or heard and feeling misunderstood, especially for my intentions, and he zeroed right in like a hawk on my vulnerable spots.

He must have realized it drove me nuts because he did it all the time. Anything to get a rise out of me so he could feel in control. He was manipulating me and I was falling for it every time.

Every night he would go to bed around 9 p.m., a couple of hours earlier than I did. I'd stay up until at least 11 just to get some time alone away from him. Just before he would retire I could feel a stillness in the office air. I would freeze up the second he turned his head to look over at me, anticipating that predictable and unnatural-sounding phrase he repeated every single night.

"Going to bed now," always delivered in the same sing-songy way, but with his robotic inflection, followed by a quick peck on the cheek.

"Can you switch it up, Fabio? Maybe say Goodnight… I'm tired… Coming to bed? Anything else?"

He slept on his back with his elbow bent, the back of his forearm resting across his forehead. I called it the *"Woe is Me"* sleeping position because it fit his personality. At 11 p.m. I would crawl into bed next to him and the minute I fell asleep that arm would straighten, fall to the side and inevitably smack me wide awake, something he continued to say was accidental.

Because he went to bed two hours earlier than I did, he would wake up at 4 or 5 a.m., jump out of bed and turn all the lights on.

"Fabio, *pleease* turn the lights out! Can you be quieter?"

"*Whaat?*"

After 10 years of that, I demanded separate bedrooms. He snored too, like a bear, but denied it.

"You're making that up!"

"Huh? Why would I make that up? And how can you say that you don't snore if you're asleep?"

Try as I might be sensitive to his ego, I found myself stepping on landmines again and again. I never wanted to hurt him, or really anyone for that matter. I am empathetic to others' needs and put theirs ahead of my own. I'm sure that's why he chose me; from the very first time that Layla and I accidentally met at his condo and I made the grave error of leaving when she cried, rather than stay and stand up for myself. Boundaries have always been a major challenge for me and I would subjugate myself to keep the peace.

Before we moved in together I had a single framed photo of Steven Tyler and me doing the tango in Houston, displayed in my Manayunk home. After we moved in together I discreetly placed it in an obscure location on the lowest shelf in the den, hidden behind the couch so as not to trigger Fabio's insecurities. He'd already shown how jealous he was of my male friends and I was determined to prove to him that I was sensitive to his needs. None of the many gold or platinum records

I was awarded back in my radio days were hung on the walls but it just didn't matter; he would still accuse me of living in the past, in the '80s.

I eventually put away every single shred of evidence from my rock & roll days, while his high school swimming trophies and framed photos from his years on the swim team remained proudly displayed. He accused me of needing too much attention but all I ever wanted was his. I just couldn't figure out how to get it. *Mom?*

Whenever we dined out with others he had to pick up the check. It didn't matter how many people were at the table or how expensive the bill was or if we could even afford it. In the middle of dinner, he would excuse himself to the men's room but actually go in search of our server to pay the bill in advance. Then, when the guests reached for their wallets, an I-Am-Better-Than-You-And-I-Will-Make-Sure-You-Know-It smirk appeared across his face as the waiter would say, "Oh, the bill's already been paid, that gentleman over there got it." On the surface it seems like a nice thing to do but his motivation was purely selfish; he had to look like a big shot, the rich guy. The image he portrayed to the outside world was everything.

All three of his brothers were completely bald. Brother Milo actually looked pretty damn sexy without hair but my husband needed to show how much more virile he was and being the only brother with hair was extremely important to that end. He even took a daily medication called Propecia to ensure he would keep his.

"You guys should have listened to me. If you'd taken this med like I told you to, you'd still have your hair!"

Well, he took that med every single day since he was 24 years old but aging is inescapable and inevitably his hairline began to recede. This was not going to work for Fabio so the only answer now was hair transplants. Two operations and $60,000 later he had hair again, but he had to lie to them about it.

He had no friends, at least none that he spent time with or called on the phone. "You have so many great qualities, Fabio. Why wouldn't someone want to be your friend?"

"Well, when you put it that way (*smirk*)," but he never even tried. There was always some excuse for not reaching out.

"I drive an hour-and-a-half to my job, my work friends all live in Jersey."

But he didn't socialize with them after work, or on the weekends. He did frequently mention how awesome everyone at R.O.U.S. thought he was though. "I'm too busy renovating the house, you need me to be here." *No, I don't.* I would beg him to involve himself in activities outside the home; maybe he could meet someone he enjoyed spending time with, and the burden of entertaining him and trying to cheer him up would not all fall on me. Besides, I needed regular breaks from his negativity, but he couldn't initiate friendships due to his fear of rejection.

R.O.U.S Industries sent him traveling all over the world, which was when I would get my breaks; someone had to stay home and take care of the house and the pets, right? Of course, we could have hired someone to house-sit, but I happily offered to do it and defer my travel dreams to our retirement years. There would always be about a week of work, training international employees on various software systems, followed by another week of vacation. That gave me two weeks of peace and quiet at home and sometimes up to a month.

He visited the ancient Incan city of Machu Picchu in Peru, the temple of Angkor Wat in Cambodia, Beijing's Great Wall, dove the Great Barrier Reef, and visited Istanbul, Shanghai, Moscow, Italy, Amsterdam, Malaysia, Colombia, and Vienna, and took multiple trips to Paris. All without me. In Paris, he discovered an underground bar that stayed open all night with musicians performing and people dancing on the bar. That sounded like fun to me; I could picture him genuinely enjoying himself. "I want to go!" "As you wish," he promised to take me once we retired.

On his drive home from the airport, he'd call to let me know he was on his way. "Do you need me to stop at the grocery store to pick anything up for you?"

"No, I'm good. I just want you to get home. I miss you."

I really did miss him. Absence makes the heart grow fonder and after a month apart I was eager to see him and hear about his trip. An hour or more later he'd casually stroll through the door with a big bag of groceries.

"I thought you were coming right home. I've been worried that something happened to you."

"I stopped at the grocery store."

I was confused; the way he'd worded it made me think that he was only going to stop if I needed something.

"Why then don't you say, 'I'm stopping at the grocery store to get myself something for dinner tonight. While I'm there, do you need anything?' That way I won't expect you or worry that you've been in an accident." He continued to do this, every single time he returned from a trip, and I continued to be frustrated that I couldn't get him to understand.

Whenever he went shopping alone I would ask him, "Please don't buy me any wine. I need an alcohol break." Despite my request, he would come home carrying two bottles of my favorite wine, Gascon Malbec, grinning, and promising to hide them from me. It wasn't until much later that I came to realize he was keeping me anesthetized so he could get away with his bad behavior and then accuse me of overusing alcohol and drugs. It was just another way of weakening me and making me dependent on him so I wouldn't abandon him.

I asked him to teach me things like how to back up my computer so I wouldn't have to bother him all the time, or how to coordinate the four different TV remotes we had. "As you wish," he lied, but conveniently never got around to showing me. "As you wish," he would say, but it never really was as I wished it would be.

Like my dad, he used a lot of canned phrases that I misconstrued to fit the narrative I held in my head. When speaking of marriage, he would declare, "Would you rather be right or would you rather be happy?" I took this to mean that he didn't want to fight and really, who does? I'd be dead wrong about that. Clearly, he preferred to be right and he loved to fight. When we did argue, even if he knew he was wrong, the best he could do for an apology was to scream at me while running in the opposite direction. "Alright already, I'm sorry!"

I realize now how I was set up and that his motivations to drive me crazy were intentional. Word salad is a clever tactic, used by narcissists to manipulate their partners. It's verbal assassination, a form of gaslighting,[43] intended to keep their victims living in a state of confusion and self-doubt.

"I never said that."

---

[43] "Gaslighting" • Psychological manipulation of a person over an extended period of time that causes the victim to question the validity of their own thoughts, perception of reality, or memories and typically leads to confusion, loss of confidence and self-esteem, uncertainty of one's emotional or mental stability, and a dependency on the perpetrator.

"That never happened."

"You're making that up."

"That wasn't my intention." Well then, what was your intention? "Not that."

"You're always bringing up the past. I don't want to be judged on past behavior, even if it was five minutes ago."

That last one always made me crazy. That meant he shouldn't be held responsible for anything, ever.

"Do you know how lucky you are to have me, Fabio? No one else in the world would put up with this shit!" As if I was somehow supposed to.

He would roll his eyes at me, constantly. When I would ask him, "Did you just roll your eyes at me?" he would say his contact had just folded over, all by itself. I can laugh about it now. His alternate response was, "I thought I saw a fly on the ceiling." OMG, here comes that damn fly again! I wondered if it was the same fly, following me from one bad marriage to another.

Regardless of the obvious signs not to, I wanted to trust him. It was foolish of me, but I knew I was trustworthy and assumed everyone was just like me. That's a pretty immature way to think. "People who have nothing to hide, hide nothing," he would say, but worded it in such a clever way, I believed he was aligning himself with the honorable side of this statement, the side of integrity. It was the "other people" who shouldn't be trusted. I guess I just wanted my husband to value honesty and have morals as I did.

When he was being avoidant, which was always, I chalked it up to his being coy, but it was definitely more like sly. He used private browsers that didn't track the websites he visited but made it seem like it was just the "smart thing" to do. He'd learned as an I.T. expert that people can hack into your computer remotely. There were secret P.O. boxes too; I'll never know what they were for but he assured me it was just another "smart thing."

Because I trusted him I allowed him to manage our finances. I had my own checking account from before we were married but he handled the joint and retirement accounts. It felt like someone was looking out for me, helping out with the minutiae of life, but in actuality, he was looking out for himself and kept the passwords private. Each month I would ask to see where we were financially. I like to plan and dream and look ahead to the time when we would retire and really begin to enjoy life. He would only let me see the balance while looking over his shoulder.

One time he tried to distract me and put me off because he'd pulled $300K from our retirement account without telling me first. Warren Buffett had mentioned a possible future crash and Fabio was always making unilateral decisions like that. It triggered memories of my childhood when my parents would do this to me… giving away my cat and moving us out of New York City. When asked why he hadn't discussed it with me or why I wasn't allowed access to the accounts, he said it was because he was afraid I'd steal it all and leave him. *Me? Nah, I'm trustworthy.* Projection[44] turned inside out and a veiled confession of who he was and what he would do, if given the chance.

"You don't consider me, Fabio! I don't feel loved by you, my opinion doesn't matter, I don't feel cherished, or trusted. Why are you like this?"

What was wrong with my husband? Why was he so arrogant? Why is he mean to me? Secretive? Why does he keep to himself, run away during a disagreement? I started researching avoidant behavior and stumbled upon Attachment Disorders and chalked it up to Avoidant Attachment Disorder.[45] It made sense to me due to the stories he told about his mom, ducking under her arm and running out of the house whenever she tried to talk to him. *Maybe he had a problem with women. I could fix that. If he doesn't trust women I will prove to him that I am trustworthy.*

I began to realize that giving him control of things had been a bad idea because he had to control everything. If I was at the wheel of the car he would clutch the handle above the door and hit phantom brakes, even though I'd always

---

[44] "Projection" • Accusing someone else of what the accuser themselves is doing.

[45] "Avoidant Attachment Disorder" • An insecure attachment characterized by an avoidance of feelings, emotional closeness, and intimacy that forms in infancy and early childhood, and extends into adulthood.

been a safe driver with no accidents on my record. He was a tailgater and a road-rager, who would drive full speed ahead to a traffic light and hit the brakes so hard all the passengers would lunge forward in their seats. His vision was poor and he couldn't see to drive at night so he drove with his chin on the steering wheel peering through the darkness, but I was not to say a thing. If I flinched, I would get 'the look.'

Still, I wanted it to be good so I kept my focus on the positive. We did have a lot of fun doing things we both loved, attending Broadway shows and so many great concerts. We adored Peter Gabriel and saw him perform many times. I was the Aerosmith fan but he enjoyed them too and bought us tickets for every single tour that came through Philadelphia. We became members of Prince's fan club to purchase VIP tickets. The *Musicology* tour took us to the St. Pete Times Forum in Tampa where we both stood front row with our elbows on the stage; we were THAT close to His Purple Badness. My friends from my Santa Barbara days made sure we always got backstage to hang with the legend Brian Wilson, of the Beach Boys, whenever he came to town.

Fabio's favorite band of all time was the Rolling Stones. Keith Richards was his hero, but Fabio had never seen them live. I'd seen them lots of times and didn't want to spend $600 a ticket for any show but he had to go, so we went. I sang along to "Jumpin' Jack Flash," danced and swayed, and tried to get him to sing and dance with me but nope, he just stood there like a totem pole, emotionless, eyes to the stage for the entire concert. At the end of the show, I asked him, "Did you even enjoy it? Was it worth the $1,200?" His deadpan response… "Yes." I wished he could show his emotions, so we could truly share these amazing experiences.

Like any normal married couple, we took an annual vacation. I let him plan every detail from booking flights and choosing hotels to scheduling the activities we did once we arrived. He loved making all the decisions, and I loved having someone take the lead. It made me feel loved and cared for and special in every way. He was the perfect tour guide and dive buddy; I trusted him completely while underwater.

One of our earliest trips was to Nassau, Bahamas. Stephen and I had visited Nassau but we stayed close to town. Fabio rented a moped and we explored the entire island, my arms wrapped around his waist, long brown hair flying in the wind. We sped by local children wearing plaid shorts and jumpers, playing in the schoolyard, and discovered a remote bay on the far side of the island with an abandoned home overlooking the water, and snuck inside. I was lucky not to fall through the rickety floorboards, but that view of the ocean from the second floor took my breath away and further solidified my dream to retire at the beach. There were piles of conch shells surrounding the house. I lifted one to my ear to hear the sound of the ocean and quickly stuffed it into my backpack. We tried sneaking them through customs but were caught. Regardless, the trip was memorable and romantic.

Scuba diving is great fun once you're below the surface but suiting up and trying to walk with all that heavy equipment hanging off me was always a challenge. Even jumping off the boat or lowering myself under the water by a knotted rope at the back of the boat caused me to panic. My strong and talented husband stayed right by my side until I was safely under the surface of the water and breathing through my regulator.

Eventually, I became more comfortable, and rather than go with a group following a divemaster, we would dive together, just the two of us. In Curaçao, we suited up on the beach and strolled right in; that was my favorite dive experience. About 10 feet off the shoreline the depth went from just a few feet to a 50-foot drop with a rock cliff covered in coral and teeming with schools of colorful fish. On that trip, we dove with a dolphin named Annie, not in a pen, but out in the open sea and I even got to pet her!

Ever since I was a kid, I'd wanted to visit the Grand Canyon. I thought the kids would dig it too so on this trip we all flew, Layla and Julian included, to Las Vegas first. I wanted to show them the disparity in this country, between overindulgence and one of the great natural wonders of the world. We stayed at the Paris Las Vegas hotel and saw Cirque du Soleil's jaw-dropping show, *Ka*, before renting a car for the 40-mile drive to our first stop, an industrial wonder of the world, Hoover Dam. After exploring the inner workings of the dam, we hopped back in the car for the next leg, to stay at the Bright Angel Lodge, perched on the South Rim of the Grand Canyon, a breathtaking spectacle everyone should witness at least once in their life.

We could have walked the 10-mile trail from the canyon rim all the way down to the river but I'd always wanted to do the mule ride, so we mounted our mules and embarked on the five-and-a-half-hour expedition down the steep canyon wall to the bottom. It was scary and thrilling and Julian almost got thrown, but we made it there alive. Traversing the iconic Black Suspension Bridge[46] spanning the Colorado River, I was awestruck by the magnificent panorama I saw before me and hoped the kids were equally impressed. Glamping at the historic Phantom Ranch on the east side of Bright Angel Creek[47] was rustic fun. What a great adventure for a little girl who'd grown up in the concrete jungle of New York City. Even Layla enjoyed herself!

In addition to bringing our kids together to form a family, we both had pets before we met. I brought along two cats, Brick and Maggie, named for the characters in Tennessee Williams' *Cat on a Hot Tin Roof*, and he had the world's best dog, Bella, a sweet and demure Rottweiler who boofed instead of barked. Brick was a stealth hunter; he loved his new home in the woods and spent most of his time outdoors, snatching birds right out of the sky and bringing home various rodents as gifts. Brick and

---

[46] "Black Suspension Bridge" • One of only two bridges spanning the Colorado River in the Grand Canyon (aka Kaibab Trail Suspension Bridge).

[47] "Bright Angel Creek" • An aquatic feature along the Southern Grand Canyon.

Maggie both lived for 17 years and Bella made it to 10. Fabio buried her along the side of the driveway of our Mount Misery home.

After Bella died I tried to gently persuade him to get another dog but he said he wasn't ready. Four years later, when I couldn't wait any longer, I suggested maybe we could adopt a baby from China. Lol! Suddenly, he was ready for another dog.

Enter Sarah, the crazy Vizsla, who wouldn't come when he called. He would grumble under his breath, "I HATE that dog," every single day until I was forced to rehome her.

He agreed to try one last time but only big dogs would be allowed. I could choose; it just had to be big. "No little yappers." I flipped through a book he had of dog breeds and stopped at one page, "What is that? That is the most beautiful dog I've ever seen!"

"That is a Bernese Mountain Dog… you've never seen one before?"

"No, never. I want one, please!"

Enter Calle, the most beautiful and fluffiest dog in the whole wide world. We adored her; she was a big bundle of love.

At times, I really thought we had a great marriage. He knew I loved donuts so for one birthday he surprised me with a donut birthday cake. Donuts were what I ate to gain 70 pounds while back in high school so once I'd lost that weight I was forced to make a rule about them… *Thou art not allowed to seek a donut but if a donut finds you, you are allowed to partake in said donut.* The donut cake qualified as "finding me" so I *allowed* myself to eat the entire thing.

Good/bad, up/down, back/forth,
thoughtful/thoughtless,
nice, and then…
mean…

Psychological manipulators will use intermittent reinforcement to keep their victims disoriented. It's a brilliant coercive tactic and it works.

During arguments he would call me a black-and-white thinker and I would look at him, puzzled. *It's YOU who's the black-and-white thinker, not me, I'm all gray. It's always all or nothing with you, like I'm for you or against you, but never in between.*

He would say that he didn't mean what he said when he was angry but I knew the truth. I wish I knew about projection back then. At one time or another, he confessed everything right to my face and it went over my head because of my cognitive dissonance. I believed what I wanted to believe so I didn't have to accept that I was caught up in a cyclone of abuse.

Projection is the narcissist's triple whammy. Take note, because they will accuse <u>you</u> of whatever it is <u>they</u> are doing. It serves several needs of the narc. One, they put you on the defense so you feel the need to defend yourself; they enjoy watching you squirm. Two, it's another form of gaslighting. You're NOT cheating or lying but you're being accused of it. It messes with your brain because you don't understand where it's coming from. And three, it gives them a great sense of superiority to confess their sins right to your face, and have you not "catch it."

How did I survive this onslaught of punishment? I was trained from a very young age not to trust my gut. My survival brain is strong and my cognitive dissonance skills are unparalleled. I'm a practical thinker. I practiced yoga four or five days a week, his traveling gave me needed breaks, and I maintained my friendships. I had a large circle of friends from before we'd met, more than he could triangulate, and my friends reported feeling that he didn't like them anyway, or approve of their friendship with me. It didn't matter; they didn't really like him either. He was on my turf, thanks to Laura moving him from Florida to Pennsylvania. I would never have survived him if we lived in Florida.

They say 50% of marriages end in divorce and 50% of those who remain married are unhappy. *Well, Erin, I guess you aren't lucky in love. Your parents weren't happy.* And then, to make myself feel better… *You've had a good career, excellent health, and wonderful friends. Life isn't fair, right? It's okay. Be grateful for what you <u>do</u> have.* These are the messages that ruminate in my brain and travel the road of what's known as the Default Mode Network.[48] Your neural pathways are set at a very young age and it's difficult to break out of them. It's like walking through a field of tall grass but with a well-worn dirt pathway right in front of you. You could go in any direction but you don't; you just follow the same path over and over again.

---

[48] "Default Mode Network" • A large-scale brain network most active when a person is not focused on external input and the brain is at "wakeful rest," i.e., daydreaming and mind-wandering.

15.
ROCK & ROLL AFTER SCHOOL: 2008-2018

The middle school years had been difficult for my son, Julian, who is about the sweetest soul you will ever meet. He'd been teased at school as early as Pre-K. His dad and I tried a private Quaker Friends school, a tough, uniformed Philadelphia public school, and finally enrolled him in the "Best School District in the State of Pennsylvania," or so said *U.S. News & World Report*. Upon graduating from the prestigious Tredyffrin/Easttown district, he could write his own ticket going forward and the school officials reminded us of that regularly.

After his dad sued me for shared custody and changed his schedule to split his weeks in half every Wednesday, Julian became even more anxious and vulnerable to bullies. The middle school recommended private therapy and included him in their "Lunch Bunch" group to keep him separated from larger groups of kids who may target him during recess when the students outnumbered the teachers 25 to one.

I was feverishly in search of activities and smaller group settings where he could feel safe and learn to thrive… Tae Kwon Do, computer camps, art classes, writing groups. I was on a mission and one day the answer just fell into my lap.

Back in 2003 when I was managing David Fagin's band, The Rosenbergs, I'd booked a gig at The Fire in downtown Philadelphia. When I arrived, the club was jam-packed; I was completely thrilled. Hundreds of people were going to see my band!

I snaked my way through the crowd to the front row and what did I see? You'll never believe it! Six kids on stage ages 8 – 14 totally rocking a Black Sabbath cover! The eight-year-old twin singers both wore Mohawks and the kids were playing their own instruments. It was astounding and I instantly thought, *this is the perfect thing for Julian!* I couldn't wait to tell him all about it the next day. He yawned, "What? I guess." I wasn't going to give up. Being in a rock & roll band teaches you all the same life skills that sports does and I personally believe that many more of the subtle nuances of life can be learned through sharing music with others. I was determined to convince him.

Lo and behold, I heard that they were just putting the finishing touches on a documentary about the Paul Green School of Rock program and told Julian we were going to go see it. I took him to the premiere at Ritz at the Bourse and after the movie we spoke to Paul Green himself.

"Hey, I bet you want me to teach your kid!" he said, boastfully.

Hmm, maybe not you, I thought to myself, but I definitely wanted him in the program and once Julian had seen the movie with the kids having so much fun, he was all in. I took him for a visit and we signed him up on the spot. He spent the next six years there learning to play the piano and guitar, and eventually took up singing lead vocals, performing the songs of his rock & roll and prog-rock heroes. He learned everything there is to learn about Frank Zappa, and that's never a bad thing.

Fast forward to 2008. I'd been working a job, not a passion, for Comcast as their Office Manager in the ticketing division. My first boss there, Fred, was a gem but my next boss made me want to quit every day.

I kept thinking about my next career move and I wanted to create a school like the School of Rock that would help kids gain confidence, make friends, and learn valuable life skills. It had helped my son so much and what I didn't realize at the time was that I was still trying to help little inner Erin. I talked it over with Fabio and decided to approach the President & CEO of School of Rock with an offer to do a franchise, but where the kids would learn real music theory so they could write their own original songs.

"We don't do that," he said, sharply. "We have a working formula."

I left heartbroken and ran away from the meeting in tears. When I arrived home I told Fabio what happened and he replied, "You don't need them, do your own thing."

Huh? What? I can do my own thing? How? Really? I can? At times like these, he truly was my prince. I felt heard by him and he put every effort into helping me make that dream a reality. I could never have done it without him. He helped me write a business plan, and cosigned a second mortgage on our home to fund the building of my very own children's music school which I called Rock & Roll After School. It would be a safe haven for kids, a sort of community recreation center where they could hang out with other like-minded kids and learn some super cool skills that would help them build confidence and develop a strong sense of self. Oh look at that, did you catch that again? Erin trying to save Erin by saving other people's teenage daughters. I guess I've done a lot of that in my lifetime. Give me a broken bird; I know just what to do.

After a year of planning and searching for the perfect location I settled on an undeveloped warehouse space about 4 miles from our home, in Phoenixville, 30 miles west of Philadelphia.

My mom lent us $50,000 and we borrowed another $200,000 against the equity in our home to build out the facility. Fabio had the idea to add another $70,000 to our obligation to eliminate the credit card debt he brought into the marriage but blamed on his ex. Sure, he was getting something out of this deal but he also allowed me to dig us a very deep financial hole believing I would be successful and that we would pull ourselves out of it. I have to say it again – at times he was my prince and this was definitely one of those times.

Not only did Fabio support my dream to build a music school for kids, he built it with his own two hands. My brother Chris, Fabio, and I cleaned out the industrial warehouse space we'd rented, dug out grease-laden trenches, poured concrete to fill them in, hammered framing, hung drywall, painted 18-foot ceilings – you name it – and after six months we finally opened Rock & Roll After School in June of 2009.

To celebrate the opening of the school, I threw a huge party in late July to coincide with my 50th birthday. I was jazzed to finally be able to share the realization of the school and wanted to show all my friends and family everything we had accomplished. Over 100 people were in attendance. Many of the area's local musicians agreed to perform as well as some of the instructors I'd hired to teach the kids. Even a few very talented new students performed. Friends flew in from all over the country to celebrate with me. I'd never been prouder of myself. It had been scary to open my own business and I knew I couldn't have done it without the support of my talented husband.

On the night of the party, Fabio offered to pick up the pizzas we'd ordered to feed everyone. To ensure they stayed hot, he made multiple trips to and from the pizza shop, so I could relax and enjoy the musical performances and spend time with our guests. I was on top of the world that night; my dream of helping children learn to write their own songs and play their own music had finally come to fruition.

As the evening came to a close, everybody gathered together near the stage to sing "Happy Birthday" to me. Fabio presented me with a birthday cake and asked me to blow out the candles. When I looked down at the icing on the cake I saw it was decorated to look like an AARP card. *Hmm.* Not very romantic and not at all what a 50-year-old woman wants to see as she's getting older. I dismissed the sinking feeling in my gut and told myself that he's just a guy and didn't mean anything by it, but it felt like a sting and I wished it had said something more flattering, like 50 & Fabulous.

Once the school was open and we had staff and customers, I began to notice that Fabio didn't interact with anyone there – not the staff members, not even the parents or the kids. I took it to mean he didn't want to steal the spotlight from me, although I truly wanted to share all of this with him. He would walk around the school with his head down, not making eye contact with anyone. People thought he was the maintenance guy. Our Music Director called him "Mr. Approachable," sarcastically, of course. His vibe was intimidating and it made everyone uncomfortable; no one even realized he was my husband. I would ask him to be friendlier with the people at the school. His response? "But if I talk to people, then I won't get anything done." His responses always sounded plausible and made him out to be the self-sacrificing good guy, making it difficult to challenge him on anything.

Granted, he was busy doing a lot for me. He did live sound for hundreds of performances, taught himself how to program the stage lights, and managed all of the equipment repairs. Did I mention that his talents also include website publishing and email marketing design? He saved us a ton of money doing all of the legal work himself, the contracts for our employees, as well as the trademark and corporate filings. I always thought we were great business partners. I was the customer service and PR side and he was the legal, tech side. It was perplexing to me. Why couldn't we get along at home?

Me: Fabio, I don't feel close to you. I wish we were closer.

Him: You're making that up!

Me: (exasperated) Why would anyone make something like that up?

Him: To prove your point!

Me: What? What point?

Him: That we don't belong together.

Once the school was up and running we grew quickly from word-of-mouth advertising. It was a lot to keep up with the demand for lessons. The original location we'd chosen was the site of an old, abandoned manufacturing plant that was being renovated by a property development group owned by a local attorney and his wife. They had no previous experience doing a commercial venture so the lease they provided did not allow for a method to calculate any increase in taxes based on the increased property value. Once they'd renovated the building, their taxes increased tenfold and they tried to pass it along to the tenants without the legal right to do so. Fabio leapt into action. "I'll take care of it," he said. "Let me explain it to them." I figured he understood the lease language and the law better than I did and trusted him to negotiate the best outcome for us.

Unbeknownst to me, this was another opportunity for Fabio to do his little triangulation trick again. He would tell me one thing, tell them another, then sit back and watch us go at each other's throats. Stuff like this was sport for him, totally entertaining, and in the end we ended up in court with the landlords and had to move the school to a new location costing us another $100,000. Just like during the family court hearings with my first husband, Fabio pretended to be supporting me when in truth he hated me to the core. He *truly* did. He resented me for having all the things he did not, a circle of friends, and an internal happiness that would not quit.

Somehow, we survived it all and enjoyed another six years of success in a much larger and much nicer facility. This one even had a basketball court for the kids to get a little exercise!

The lawsuit and subsequent move took its toll on both of us. It was around this time that Fabio bought an early version of a vape, called a Volcano[49] and we began smoking marijuana on a daily basis. Because our kids didn't know we smoked, we would sit on the tile bench inside the master bedroom shower with the exhaust fan on high. Our alcohol consumption increased until we were drinking almost every day. Substance abuse is a signal of the deep underlying anxiety that the narcissist feels at all times. Our cork collection grew large enough to build a small boat or raft in the future. He filled trash bag after trash bag with them and stored them in the basement.

I never felt like I could say anything critical to him; he'd worked so hard on our behalf and was still working at R.O.U.S. Industries during the week. The new school was three times the size of our original location and required many more hours of our time. I was the face of the school and worked on-site six days a week, but he spent many hours on the weekends taking care of all the things I couldn't do.

One day we were both at the school and a customer approached me to ask if I would "bend the rules" for him. He was a "good customer" and "shouldn't be held to the rules." The rules were pretty simple; we asked for 24 hours' notice to reschedule a lesson and he'd forgotten to notify us in advance. I reminded him that the policies are in place to protect the instructors. As independent contractors, they are paid per lesson and rely on that

---

[49] "Volcano Vaporizer" • An electromechanical device designed to vaporize chemical compounds from plant material or oils by means of heated air.

notice to project their income and manage their personal budgets. He escalated immediately and demanded I make an exception for him.

"You're always throwing policy in my face," he yelled, loud enough for everyone in the school to hear him. I tried to keep my cool and looked over at Fabio who was, as usual, even cooler, staying out of it and watching this guy go at me. I pleaded with Fabio, through my eyes, please help me! I need you to step in and step up for me, but he never did. He got off on it.

Whenever the instructors gathered in the front of the school to shoot the shit at the end of the night, I would look around and wonder where my husband had disappeared to. I'd go looking for him and usually found him sitting right on the other side of the wall behind my office, seemingly oblivious to the staff.

"Why don't you join us, Fabio?"

"Uh, I didn't know where you were."

"What? We're 10 feet away."

I felt disconnected from him and even more so from myself. This was *supposed* to be fun. I reached out to him again and again, trying to feel connected, but Fabio was not a talker and suddenly my strong, silent partner felt like a complete stranger to me. Every night on my ride home I would call to tell him what had happened that day. Once I'd shared a cute story or two about the students' successes I would then ask him, "What have you been up to?" *Pause*.

Him: Nothing.

Me: Nothing? I've been at work for seven hours. Nothing?

Him: Uh, work, I guess.

Me: Is that all? It's nine o'clock.

Him: Uh, I ate dinner.

Me: What did you have for dinner?

I was desperately trying to make a connection with him.

Him: Uh, chicken. Aren't you going to be home soon (sounding like he wanted to get off the phone)?

Everything with him was like pulling teeth so I finally gave up calling him on my ride home from work.

He never wanted to share with me and it hurt me deeply. The best he could do to keep a phone call going was to say after each story I would share, "Anything else? Anything else?" in a robotic voice. I'd heard this phrase before, whenever Layla would call him, and she would struggle to think of another story to tell him. After "Anything else? Anything else?" he ended every phone call with her the same way, "Always love you, Pookie."

Granted, it sounds sweet, the words are right, the sentiment seems to be there, but his robotic delivery and lack of inflection made it feel disingenuous. Narcs don't divulge personal information about themselves. They collect ammunition, disguised as interest, to use against you later. Every Christmas Layla would ask me what to get him because he never talked about himself. Most Christmases, he got a cigar, and one year she gave him pancake mix.

Even with all the challenges we faced both professionally and personally, the school was a huge success. It did exactly what it was created to do – it helped kids learn to be kids in a world that seems to have forgotten how important those developing years are. There are nearly 1,000 videos on YouTube of original songs written by children ages 7 – 18 that would never have existed without all the work we put into creating the school.

In the 10 years Rock & Roll After School was in operation we positively impacted the lives of thousands of kids and teens while saving countless from self-harm. I took everything about the school personally and spent each and every day there sitting in my office, talking with kids about their lives, trying to help guide them toward healthier choices.

In 2014 I was invited to do a TEDx talk about my program as a part of "Sex, Drugs and Rock & Roll, It's Not What You Think," held in Phoenixville. With our elite, touring group of students sitting in a semi-circle around me, each one of them staring down at their phones, I delivered the 20-minute talk, "Give a Kid an Instrument, Not a Device," followed by a resounding performance by the kids featuring my old friend, the talented and 'too good looking for Fabio' Eric Bazilian, who delivered his own magnificent TEDx talk that day. At the conclusion of the musical performance, the audience of 600 were on their feet, cheering. It was one of my proudest achievements.

16.
BUILDING THE BOCAS HOUSE: 2012–2018

We'd worked so hard and for so long and were preparing to retire, finally (*whew!*), and realize the fruits of our labor. I always dreamed of returning to my hometown of New York City, with a little beach house somewhere in New England, maybe even on Cape Cod.

I imagined us frequenting all of the city's great museums, attending performances at Jazz at Lincoln Center, and becoming members of the Metropolitan Opera. We would try out all the great restaurants, and take advantage of everything the Big Apple has to offer. It's easy to get around without a car. We'd go on long strolls together through Central Park and I'd have lunch with the ladies. Surrounded by airports that could take us anywhere in the world we wanted to go, he would finally take me to that little underground cabaret he'd visited in Paris, where they stay up all night singing and dancing on the bar. It seemed the perfect answer to "where should we retire?" Fabio went along with my idea so I contacted a friend who was a real estate agent and she set up several appointments for us to see what was available within our budget.

We made several trips to Manhattan and visited many beautiful apartments in the most desirable neighborhoods. Only one problem – once you added the condo fees the bottom-line cost nearly doubled and my dream of retiring to Manhattan seemed like less and less of a possibility. "When do I get to stop working?" he begged me. I knew he was right and it didn't seem fair after all his hard work, so I resigned myself to the fact that I'd missed my chance to move back to New York. *We could always visit.*

He had another idea. A few years earlier, he'd visited Layla while she was studying abroad in Costa Rica. They'd taken a diving trip to a tiny archipelago off the coast of northern Panama called Bocas del Toro. Whenever we vacationed on his Hilton Honors points, I would ask if next time we could find something a little more remote, you know, where dad takes you fishing and mom cooks the fish. A high-rise hotel on an island is just plain weird.

When they landed in charming little Bocas Town and found the streets unpaved, he called me right up. "I found it," he said, "your mom and pop vacation spot."

This will make him happy, I thought. I wanted so much for him to be happy. He promised me if we could move to Bocas he finally would be. As a teen, he'd dreamed of becoming a marine biologist or an oceanographer. He admired Jacques Cousteau and even owned a small piece of his famous research vessel, the Calypso, encased in resin. He would be kinder to me in Bocas, he promised me. He would never rage or threaten me if we could only move there. The stress of living in the USA was killing him and I wanted with everything in my heart to believe him. If I couldn't have New York, living at the beach overlooking the Caribbean would be just fine with me.

We contacted an American real estate agent in Panama who showed us a variety of options. First up, an overwater bungalow with a cool breeze coming up from the water where you could fish right off the deck or dive in to cool off. He showed us a jungle lodge on 100 acres, and a tiny, open-aired cabin on the far side of the most remote island in the archipelago, with panoramic views of the ocean. There were homes high up in the hills and some right on the beach.

One day the agent suggested we ride our bikes out to Blave Beach on Isla Paloma, the main island, to see what we thought of that area. We hopped onto our rented bikes and took off on the 45-minute ride up the dirt road that hugs the shoreline, and arrived at a pristine beach with bright orange sand and competition-sized waves, a haven for nesting leatherback turtles. I loved it! Many of the expats who had retired and relocated to Bocas were living on Blave Beach, and I felt a sense of community there. I knew I needed to be around people since my husband wasn't much of a talker, and we met some super cool folks.

The Beach Bar, situated right in the sand, was the place to hang, and the bartender poured generously. It's not like anyone was driving home, just like in Manhattan. I was sold. On our ride back to Bocas Town we saw a red and white vinyl banner hanging between two trees; "Lots for Sale" it read, and we jotted down the number. "Fabio, I want to live at Blave Beach. Let's call Randy."

The following day Randy met us at Simon Bolivar Park in town and we hailed a cab out to Blave Beach to check out some properties. Riding in a cab in Bocas is always an adventure. The drivers regularly pick up and drop off locals holding chickens in their laps, with goats in the flatbed behind us poking their heads through the window and nibbling at my ears.

We stopped at the property we'd seen the day before and I climbed up to the top of the hill. As I looked out over the water facing east I noticed a little dip in between the trees that looked like an inverted slice of pizza, revealing the Caribbean Sea. OMG, *Fabio loves pizza!*

I stood on the hill, taking in the magnificent view and it felt like home. *Here! I belong here!* I felt a rush of life flow over me and imagined what it would feel like to wake up every day and practice yoga to the sunrise overlooking the Caribbean.

For the next six years, we took many trips to Panama while building our new home. We'd spend the night in Casco Viejo, the original location of Panama City, with its quaint cobblestone streets and many Catholic, gothic churches, and eateries. We sat outside for lunch, enjoying the warm weather while eating burgers at Casablanca on the Square, and imagined our happy future together.

On each trip to Panama, we dined at the most elegant and romantic restaurant called Caliope[50] (sic) and sat on a bench in the park to people watch. We stayed overnight at the Hotel Casa Antigua, a warm, Spanish Colonial–style hotel with wrought iron balconies that overlooked the bay to the magnificent silver skyscrapers of the new Panama City skyline. It took three planes to get to Bocas… Philadelphia to Miami, Miami to Panama City, then a puddle jumper from Panama City to Bocas del Toro. It was as remote as a destination can be.

Exploring the ancient neighborhoods, walking through the markets, and taking in the culture and Spanish architecture, we would break for a little respite in the tiny shops for coffee and treats, or relax in outdoor bars, our favorite being La Rana Dorada. We were learning everything we could about the area and enjoying what would soon become our new home.

There were several steps to citizenship. The first was residency, and following that Fabio obtained his Panamanian Driver's License. Our attorney led us through the immigration process like a lady shark in Jimmy Choo heels, and we eventually received our Permanent Residency cards. The reality was setting in

---

[50] "Caliope" • A landmark steakhouse in Casco Viejo, Panama. Yes, only one "L."

and I was genuinely excited for the opportunity to have a fresh start together and live a completely different lifestyle in the tropics.

We got matching pierced earrings to celebrate his retirement from R.O.U.S. Industries. Our plan was to sell the Valley Forge house and Rock & Roll After School and use the proceeds to retire together in Panama.

Our realtor recommended a local builder who took us for a ride on his boat to the various islands around the archipelago to show us some of the beautiful homes he'd built. We decided on a house built with local indigenous hardwoods, Nispero and Almendro, with hand-carved cutouts along the roofline to allow the cool ocean breeze to waft through the upstairs level of the home and back out to the thick jungle behind us. The builders called me La Jefa (pronounced Heffa), which in Spanish means Boss Lady. They checked every single decision with me. If La Jefa isn't happy, no one is happy!

As our home started to take shape, I picked out glass tiles and chose natural wood trees to support the deck overlooking the Caribbean Sea. It was shaping up to be a masterpiece and I couldn't wait to live there. I posted pictures of our progress on Facebook, and all my friends were genuinely excited for me and commented about how stunning it was.

In May of 2013, we began working with a local charity, building a school for the indigenous children in Playa Roja on neighboring Bastimentos Island. We sat and watched the children play baseball in their bare feet, sharing only one bat, one ball, and one glove. It warmed my heart to see these beautiful young faces who didn't need iPads to entertain them. I wanted to hug them all and decided that I would continue working with these children once I moved there permanently, teaching the young girls yoga and female empowerment.

We rented a 3-wheeler ATV to explore the main island, with me on the back, arms wrapped around his waist and him at the reins, just like our romantic Bahamas vacation when we collected conch shells and first talked about living on the water.

On one of these rides, my favorite hot pink Croc sandal flew off my foot and into the jungle before I even realized it was gone. A week later we found it 50 feet away from the dirt road and joked about the 'more stylish' monkeys carrying it off. We walked together for miles down the dirt road that hugged the shoreline, to the very end of the island and located the Piscina, a natural inlet where the fresh water flowed down from the hills and met with the salt water of the ocean. It was a secluded little swimming hole where you could swim naked.

We sat naked on the beach at night, breathing in the fresh air and taking in the moon that rose up over the water. No one was there on the beach, no one for miles. We discovered the old abandoned Chiquita Banana plantation just past the Piscina, the original site of the company before it was moved to the mainland. I just knew Fabio would be happy here; this is his kind of place. Everywhere you look is completely beautiful and it's always a temperate 82 degrees. And not a snow blower in sight!

We collected sprouting coconuts we found around the island and planted them to build a line of fruiting trees in the front of the property. We were both pretty artistic and planned to mosaic the front columns of the house and the sides of the bodega behind it with my sea glass collection, grandfather's WWI medals, some Monopoly pieces and other trinkets, and all the broken jewelry I'd saved for some unknown, future purpose. I'd make my mark on that land and leave a tiny piece of personal history there, like a time capsule.

The dream I'd had so long ago while sitting on the edge of the cliff in Cape Cod was finally coming true, but in a more meaningful way than I'd ever imagined. I could continue my work with children here, apprentice with a master Argentinian chef down the road, and create an off-grid permaculture[51] homestead. I studied permaculture practices for years leading up to our move so I could grow as much of our own food as possible and took beekeeping classes so we'd have our own honey. Fabio had an unnatural fear of bees but not me; I liked to pet them right in front of him, because I'm fearless, or maybe just because it freaked him out. *Wink.*

---

[51] "Permaculture" • The conscious design and maintenance of agriculturally productive ecosystems which have the diversity, stability, and resilience of natural ecosystems.

We'd stroll hand in hand, down the road to Blave Beach to watch baby leatherback turtles make their way to the sea. Fabio wanted to restore the coral reefs that were bleaching due to the shallow waters there. He'd be my Jacques Cousteau, my Crocodile Dundee. He could finally go barefoot all the time.

While overseeing the building process we frequently stayed at Joya Escondida, the little surfer hostel that hung out over the surf directly across from our future home. We explored the various islands of the archipelago and roamed the jungle behind our land. The wildlife was incredible with adorable sloths sleeping in trees, white-faced capuchin monkeys chattering to each other while traveling through our backyard, and colorful parrots and toucans, not in cages, but living in the thick rainforest.

17.
BREAST REDUCTION: AUGUST 2015

Have you ever had anyone speak to you in the third person, as if you weren't even there? This doozy happened in Panama at Joya Escondida. We had just settled in after a long day of flying.

Nothing seemed out of the ordinary that day. Fabio and I were staying in one of the small bungalows at the bottom of the hill, the one with the glass wall made from upcycled wine bottles.

I was sitting on the bed unpacking my suitcase when I became aware of a chill in the air. Feeling a chill in Panama is never a good thing. I looked up at Fabio and saw his body stiffening and that glassy look in his black eyes. I held my breath because I knew what was coming, *best to be very still so he doesn't hurt you...*

And then, seemingly out of nowhere and with no provocation, "I used to have a wife with the perfect body but now she's gone and butchered it and I have to look at other women for sexual pleasure."

"Whaat?"

He repeated it, this time louder, and more threatening. "I have to look at other women for pleasure."

"Oh, really, like who?" He then proceeded to rattle off the names of my three closest girlfriends whose breasts were big enough for him.

I'd had a breast reduction earlier that year in preparation for a life in bathing suits and spaghetti-strapped sundresses. My 32DDD breasts had been a burden all my life. They brought me unwanted attention as a young teen and now, daily back and neck pain. Insurance even paid for it all but Fabio was angry; they were his, not mine, and my feelings and need for comfort never mattered to him.

18.
RAN OVER A GUY
ON ROUTE 202 AT NIGHT:
FALL 2015

Back home again, another devastating incident occurred. It's never good news when your phone rings after midnight. I was in bed, just about to fall asleep. Fabio was driving home from visiting his daughter in DC, and a few minutes after midnight my cell phone rang. I picked it up and it was Fabio.

Him: I'm going to be a little late.

Me: Is everything alright?

Him: There's been an accident (delivered without emotion, dissociative).

Me: Are you okay?

Him: Yes.

Me: What happened?

Him: There's been an accident.

Me: Was your car involved?

Him: Yes.

Me: How's the other guy?

Him: He's dead.

Me: Oh, my God! What happened?

Him: He's under my tire. I have to go; the cops are here.

There was no going back to sleep after hearing this news. I waited an hour for him to come home and when he finally did he went straight to bed and didn't want to talk about it at all.

A week later, my mom was visiting and gently nudged him, "Hey Fabio, how are you doing?"

He replied, "Fine, why do you ask?"

Mom clarified. "I mean, since the accident."

And without emotion, Fabio matter-of-factly spoke. "Oh, that? That guy got what he deserved for riding a bike on Route 202 at night; he was in my way," and walked out of the room.

My mom and I stared at each other in disbelief… he didn't care one bit. Never gave it a second thought. My mom did me a big disservice that day when she told me,

"He just can't process the trauma," which I took to mean he was so sensitive and deeply empathetic that he had to block it out. Sadly, I was 100% wrong.

19.
GRAND MAL SEIZURE: FALL 2016

Ronnie, my close friend from New York, often came to visit us at our home in Valley Forge. Her son Adrian had been friends with Julian ever since she and I met while working at WXPN. We were both single moms, with boys of the same age totally obsessed with Pokémon. Her very large family lived nearby in Ambler and we spent every 4th of July at her parents' house watching fireworks with her six siblings, their spouses, and 50-some-odd kids.

This night, just Ronnie was over and the three of us were partying on the back deck. We had a bottle of wine or two and Ronnie was always good for some smoke. She spoke quickly at times; it was difficult to follow her. I was better at deciphering "Ronnie speak" than Fabio was, having grown up in New York where everything moves quickly. He just sat there quietly, absorbing Ronnie's somewhat manic energy until he could take it no more and excused himself from the table. It wasn't the first time he'd done this; he often went straight to bed when she would visit.

He stood up, walked through the French doors into the house, and I let Ronnie finish her story. Once she was done, we headed in behind him and found Fabio sitting on a stool at the breakfast bar, hunched over with his head down. As we entered the room he slowly stood up to offer us his seat. Grabbing onto the edge of the counter to stabilize himself, he made his way around and across the room to the kitchen sink. Leaning over the sink and clearly out of it, Ronnie asked him, "Hey Fabio, are you okay?" He began to right himself, turned his head in our direction, his voice quivering, and said, "Well, I'm *aaa…*" and in slow motion, he began to lean back, without his knees buckling beneath him, or grabbing on to anything on the way down. He hit the tile floor, the back of his head first.

Like a domino or a felled tree, it was absolutely terrifying to witness and I thought he was dead. I screamed, "Call 911!" Ronnie ran to find her phone and I ran across the room yelling, "Fabio, Fabio!" I straddled his motionless body, ready to administer CPR I'd learned from my lifeguard days when all of a sudden, his body started convulsing, and he went into a full-blown grand mal seizure. There was nothing I could do, but he was alive, thank God. When it was over, he lifted his head like nothing had happened.

"You don't need to call 911, I'm fine."

No, honey, you're going to the hospital.

The CAT scan showed no damage. I didn't know how that was possible; I'd seen evidence of head injury with him before and I thought back to my father.

Years prior, Fabio had developed a severe inner ear infection that caused him to suffer vertigo. I found him huddled in a ball in the corner of the leather couch in the den one day; he couldn't tell up from down. I literally carried him to the doctor. It wasn't easy; he was over six feet tall and weighed more than 200 pounds. The minute we entered the doctor's office he threw up. Vertigo continued to plague him and I wouldn't let him climb a ladder anymore. I recalled when we were first dating, he'd once fainted for no reason at all. Totally sober while walking to the bedroom one night, he'd fallen backward right on top of me. I brushed it off at the time but now I wonder. Like the doctors said about my dad, *had he fallen many times before?*

20.
THE SPATCHCOCK THANKSGIVING: 2016

Thanksgiving was three days away. We'd assumed our regular morning positions, side by side upstairs in our home office. I noticed in my peripheral vision an image of a turkey on his computer, and in a very compromising position, so I asked, "What is that?" No response, eyes focused forward as if he didn't hear me. I repeated, "What's that?" He stood up without saying a word and headed downstairs to the kitchen so I followed him.

I stood outside the kitchen door and watched him, one by one, yanking out each spice drawer, and then slamming it shut. I waited until he got to the bottom drawer. "What are you looking for?" I asked helpfully. He barked angrily without looking up at me, "Something that's not here!" I assured him, "I know where all the spices are and I'm happy to help you find what you need."

"I SAID, SOMETHING THAT'S NOT HERE!" and then he stomped away and around the partition wall toward the stairs.

I yelled, "STOP!" He turned around, looked me dead in the eye, and said, "You're a fucking groupie! You want to fuck Steven Tyler. You wish you were Bebe Buell."

I slapped him right across the face. I'd never hit anyone before in my life. He didn't even flinch. He turned and ran up the stairs, pushing Julian out of the way, and locking himself in the upstairs bedroom for the remainder of the day.

I began to worry about going to Bocas with him and looked for any excuse I could find not to go. I'd read news stories online about a young woman who was murdered by her boyfriend there, cut up, and placed in backpacks deep in the jungle. Then there was the story about Wild Bill, a modern-day pirate guy who murdered five expats.

"What if I miss my friends?"

"You'll get new friends," from the guy who had none.

But what about the friends I already have? I love them, I don't know if I can move away from them. My mom is ill, what if she dies while I'm in Panama? I'd never forgive myself.

I thought maybe if we purchased a condo in King of Prussia, it could become the turnkey, pied-à-terre[52] I could escape to if I needed my friends or missed my family. We found a perfect two-bedroom and renovated that too. While adding a medicine cabinet to the hall bath, Fabio accidentally drilled through a water pipe and flooded the apartment downstairs. The bill to repair their unit was over $4,000 so he blamed it on the "idiots" who constructed the building wrong, way back in 1971.

Julian needed a place to live and Calle needed a yard to play in while we fixed up the Valley Forge house to sell, so we purchased a small investment property in Lancaster. Julian contributed the $13,000 down payment and Fabio and I financed the remaining $50,000. Julian and his roommate paid us the monthly mortgage amount and took care of our furbaby for a year.

---

[52] "Pied-à-Terre" • A small apartment in a large city, used mostly as a means by which the owner can avoid the long commute to their primary residence far out of town.

21.

FABIO'S CHILDHOOD

I'm not sure what actually happened in the Venditti household while those kids were growing up in suburban DC, but just like the Rileys, it looked a whole lot better on the outside than history would eventually reveal. Among the five siblings, there've been 10 divorces and still counting. Fabio pointed to his father's passing when he was 17 years old as the reason for all of his life's troubles, but his problems clearly go back much farther than that.

Evelyn hit them with sticks. She didn't have the emotional tools to manage five kids. They would all laugh about it while reminiscing about their childhood, but I would cringe at the thought of being pummeled by my own mother. My mom kept it cool at all times. I figured they were Italian, and I guess that's more accepted than it is when you're an uptight northerner, like me. Just look at me; I can rationalize absolutely anything!

For years, he kept a box filled with Super8 movies from their childhood until the technology became available to transfer them all to digital. He spent over a year editing and compiling a separate segment for each Venditti family member, and set them all to music. I would look over his shoulder, jealous that they even had videos of their childhoods.

I have nothing like that. We didn't have the money for a video camera and our parents never seemed to care much about us anyway. I was moved to tears by the section devoted to his dad. He seemed so loving, so proud of each and every child, holding them up for all the world to see, and playing with them in the pool. I wished I'd had a dad that would hug me, and proudly show me off like his dad did. I suggested using Rod Stewart's "Forever Young" as the background music for his dad's segment, and it fit perfectly. When it came time for Fabio to work on his own, while peering over his shoulder, I noticed something very telling.

All the other kids are shown interacting with their friends. They giggle, punch each other in the arm, and run away laughing. Brother Milo is seen hamming it up for the camera every time they point it in his direction. All of the other kids look comfortable being held by their parents. All of the other kids make eye contact with others, they smile, they romp, they play. But one of them is not like the others.

Evelyn once told me, "He's always been a loner; he's never had any friends." *Geez Mom, did you think that might be a problem?* The very first time she ever visited us at our house in Valley Forge she said to me, "Have you ever noticed how negative he is?" He hadn't yet shown that side of himself to me, but in short order, I would come to know it intimately.

The family videos show a loving, normal family but the final outcomes point to some serious internal family dysfunction.

"You're a Venditti!" they told him. "You're better than other people, never forget that."

He was a picky eater from birth so his mom made him a separate meal from the rest of the family. He was treated differently than the other kids – better. The siblings resented him and he said so all the time. He shared a name with his father and would carry the burden of that name like a cross.

Dad was diagnosed with pancreatic cancer when the youngest sibling was only eight years old; my future husband – the oldest, but still only 17. Fabio and his dad were at odds at that time in his life, over things like wearing his hair long, staying out late, and smoking pot. It was the typical teen dynamic with his parents; he kept everything a secret from them and ducked under his mom's arm to escape the house if she tried to talk to him. He continued this avoidant behavior throughout both of his marriages.

His father refused all possible life-extending treatments. Due to his elite status in the community as a Federal Judge, and his mom's background in nursing, he was permitted to live at home over the three-month course of his terminal illness. Evelyn administered pain meds and he would get to spend his final weeks at home surrounded by family. All the other kids spent their evenings sitting bedside with him, listening to stories of his life. They each received a book with a personalized message inscribed on the inside cover page to guide them into adulthood without their father present.

But one of them was not like the others and avoided him the entire time he lay dying, until the final night when they were awakened by their mom to say their goodbyes. This, he said, was the root of all his problems and why he always says, "I've lived a life of guilt and regret," and the reason he could never set proper boundaries with his daughter. He made a conscious decision that he would never allow anyone close to him ever again. He would become like Spock – logical, emotionless, and cold, to protect his inner child from experiencing pain.

As the oldest, Fabio was expected to take his dad's place in the family. His uncle pulled him aside at the funeral. "I'm sorry, son. I know you're only 17, but you're going to have to step up." Evelyn was still working as a nurse and the younger kids were all still in school, involved in a variety of extracurricular activities. Young Fabio needed to drive them to swim practice each day and navigate the treacherous DC beltway as a teen driver so they could continue to compete in swim meets. Trying to fill those shoes was just too much for him to handle. His dad had been a huge presence in the community, and the patriarch of the Venditti family. He could never fill his father's shoes and remained a mid-level manager throughout his career, living under the radar, while harboring resentment and anger for the circumstances that put him there.

He blamed his father's death for everything that went wrong in his life. It was the pinnacle of his never-ending sob story. All of his emotional problems were a result of this tragic event, but I knew his first wife Laura's dad also died when she was just a teen. Her father was killed in an airplane crash and she never even got to say goodbye to him. She's not a sociopath. My dad fell down a flight of stairs when I was 17 and never fully recovered. Unable to work and collecting disability insurance for the rest of his life, he died at age 81, after yet another fall. I am not a sociopath either.

There's a Venditti family motto – "If you're not at lunch, you ARE lunch!" It always made me uncomfortable when he would say it, and I believe he said it for a reason. It's a veiled threat, directed right at me. It's not funny, not funny at all. In fact, it sounds rather "mob-like," doesn't it?

They were always backstabbing each other. Fabio bad-mouthed each and every one of his siblings but the contempt he held for his mom was beyond comprehension. Whenever she called to ask for help with her computer he would grumble under his breath, "Why does she have to call me all the time? Why doesn't she call Milo? He knows as much about computers as I do." He would hold the phone an arm's length away from his ear muttering to himself while rolling his eyes. It always made me uncomfortable. My mom's no peach, but I could never have treated her like that.

The first far-fetched story he ever told me about her was that she had been sold into sexual slavery when she was 13 years of age. Her mother had been institutionalized and young Evelyn was abandoned by both of her parents. The story eventually evolved into: she'd gone to live with an uncle when her mom was diagnosed mentally ill and no longer able to care for her. Who knows what the truth is? There are so many secrets and lies flying around in the Venditti family.

Fabio made fun of absolutely everyone he ever met and his mother was no exception. At one point, she invested money in a fly-by-night, garage-based pharmaceutical company run by two guys that promised a cure for AIDS. That story alone evoked a major eye roll from him and an evil laugh about how gullible she was. "Pie in the sky, head in the clouds," he would describe her. He joked about her lesbian love affair with Ingrid, her one-time business partner, and cackled about the "Ingrid Wall," filled with travel photos of the two of them during their many vacations together.

I will never know what is true and what is false from the stories Fabio told me. He lied so many times that it's simply impossible to know. Truth is not a thing with narcs.

He should have been my knight in shining armor. He had everything I ever wanted, ever needed, but buried too deep within him to grasp.

22.

THE MOMENT I KNEW:
EASTER 2017

It was a week before Easter. I was sitting upstairs in our home office surfing Facebook or some other random Internet waste of time when Fabio entered the room and stated that Layla would be graduating from her RCIA (Rite of Christian Initiation of Adults) classes and he wanted to attend the official ceremony for her to be indoctrinated into the Catholic church that weekend, but I was not welcome to join him. We both thought it weird that Layla so desperately wanted to become a Catholic, as though she were looking for something to belong to other than her broken family. Can't imagine why. So, here's how the conversation went:

Him: Layla is graduating from Catholic school in DC this weekend and I'm going to go, but she doesn't want you there.

Me: Why not?

Him: She says it would make her feel uncomfortable and ruin her day.

Me: Fabio, we've been together for over 17 years now, when WILL she be comfortable with me?

DRUM ROLL… his reply…

Him: Maybe another 17 years.

And in that moment, I finally knew. Yes, it took nearly 18 years for me to finally realize that his behavior was intentional and manipulative and that it would NEVER change. How ridiculous… my step-daughter "might" get used to me after perhaps 34 or more years together. The argument that followed was the turning point in our relationship. There is no going back once you realize you've been gamed like that.

"That's just ridiculous, Fabio. If you go to DC this weekend without me, I'm going on a date!"

He glared at me, defying me to do so. I'm sure he didn't believe me. Hell, I didn't believe me! Friday came and he left for DC without me.

It was Easter weekend so I drove alone to spend Saturday with Julian in Lancaster, came home after a long day, and went straight to bed.

Sunday morning, it occurred to me that I had "forgotten" to go on a date and wondered if I did, who would I "go on a date" with? Good question. I opened my browser and typed in Match.com to see what was available in my age group and geographical range and quickly closed it.

I didn't sign up for an account; I just looked at the first page of available options and decided there was no one there for me and I might as well stick with Fabio.

I then drove to my brother's in North Jersey for our annual holiday meal and some good quality time with family. I left his house in Flemington around 4 p.m. and drove the two hours home to find Fabio, arms crossed over his chest, standing tall like a totem pole right in the center of the driveway, his eyes blackened with anger. I eventually realized that he must have checked my browser history and had been tracking my phone all the way home, and up the hill to our home on Mount Misery.

I drove the car around him onto the lawn and pulled into the garage. I opened the car door to find him hovering over me, like Donald Trump looming over Hillary Clinton in their 3rd presidential debate. He followed me all through the house like that and up the stairs to the office where I sat down in my chair, turned and looked at him, and said calmly, "Can I help you?" to which he replied, "All I want to know is who is moving to the condo and who is staying here?" Me: "I'm not going anywhere," and he turned and stormed out of the house.

It was after this frightening episode that I contacted the Domestic Violence Center of Chester County, which offered me free weekly counseling with a young therapist at the Phoenixville Health Foundation, only 10 minutes from my home. Until then, I hadn't even realized I was being abused.

From that day on I never fell for his narcissistic tricks again. April 15, 2017, was the turning point in our marriage – 6,425 days after our first date, the day Fabio decided to destroy me for looking at the front page of Match, where we first met. *Ironic.*

23.
13-HOUR FIGHT #1 –
UPSTAIRS BEDROOM:
MAY 2017

Our Valley Forge realtor Kelly wanted the house ready to be put on the market by May 1st, in time to capture home buyers looking to get into the prestigious Tredyffrin/Easttown School District in time to register for the upcoming school year. My brother Chris agreed to help us get the house ready, along with his partner Larry, so I contacted him in late January to schedule, but he didn't respond. I asked Fabio if he would reach out to him directly to discuss materials that would be needed. He ignored me completely, just like always. So, I waited a few more days, and asked again; he rolled his eyes at me and ignored me once again. After a few more gentle attempts and three weeks of asking nicely, on February 26, 2017, I told him he was on his own.

I refused to nag him to get the house ready in time because I thought it would take at least eight weeks to complete the work. He didn't verbalize it to me at the time; I only received the standard eye roll, but Fabio thought it would only take two weeks and that as a woman, I didn't know anything and was, as usual, overreacting. *Ok, buddy, you're on your own*, and I went back to the condo to stay. In the end, the renovation lasted over nine weeks and we missed our May 1st deadline to get the house on the market.

Mid-renovation, I stopped by the house to drop off some paint and found my brother working in the den. I asked, "Where's Fabio?" Chris pointed to the upstairs, so I gingerly climbed the three flights of stairs to the top floor where I found him coming out of the master closet. "Can we talk?" He ignored me and tried to force his way around me, but I blocked his path to the door. I made him sit with me on the shag carpet of the bedroom floor for the next 13 hours while I interrogated him with 'why' questions, "Why this? Why that?" I needed to know everything he'd been hiding from me for the past 20 years to even consider moving to Panama with him. I didn't let him eat, pee, sleep, or leave (I didn't either) until he answered me.

Me: Why do you lie to your brothers about your hair transplants?

Him: I don't know, he sobbed.

Me: But why? They love you, Fabio, they wouldn't care.

Him: No, they hate me. They've always resented me.

Me: The shopping cart crap, Fabio, not saying 'excuse me;' that's on purpose to make other people feel stupid. You get off on that, don't you? Makes you feel superior.

Him: Yes, he cried.

It was the most painful day of our marriage but I finally got some of the answers I'd been looking for, for almost 20 years.

I've pulled a lot of teeth with Fabio over the years but nothing was like this day. It was like his mouth was sewn shut and inside he was in an internal war with himself saying, NO, DON'T TRUST HER, DON'T TELL HER THE TRUTH, DON'T TELL HER ANYTHING! IT'S A TRICK. I will never know if these stories are true but if they are, I know how and when my husband experienced a psychotic break and retreated inward, never growing a single year older emotionally after that.

By the time we left the room it was close to midnight and my brother and Larry were long gone, but I finally had the pieces of the puzzle I'd been asking for to begin to understand what happened to my husband to make him a covert narcissist.

So, here's the story and my understanding of its effect on him:

In 9th grade, in the showers on the first day of gym class, he was brutally teased by the other boys about his "size," or lack thereof. The next day, his daddy, the Federal Judge, came to the school and wrote him out of gym class for the next four years stating that he swam during the summers and did not need to be humiliated at school. Well Dad, guess what you just did? No high school girlfriends for

Fabio, ever. The only safe place to try and get laid was at the pool where he was the swim coach and a lifeguard. Unfortunately, word travels, and one day at the pool Fabio overheard two teen girls talking.

"Hey, how about that cute lifeguard?"

The other: "Don't bother, tiny dick."

And lastly, he'd had a crush on a girl at the pool named Christine. After waiting three years, she agreed to date him for the final two weeks of summer, but no sex. She said she liked him too much and wanted to wait… except, on Labor Day weekend, she attended a party without him, got drunk, and had sex with "at least six different guys."

Fabio's deepest shame is related to the size of his penis. He hates all men because they have a bigger one than he does. He hates all women because they want them.

This was the hardest conversation I've ever had with another person, but it left me with more hope for our future than I'd ever had before. If these stories are actually true, Fabio may have gifted me with a little glimpse into the inside of his fragile heart. I'd waited almost 20 years for him to show his true self to me, his vulnerable side… the truth. *This will be the turning point for us,* I thought to myself, *we might actually make it now.* All I ever wanted from him was the truth.

Sadly, Fabio had the opposite reaction. *I've told her too much, she's going to use it against me now. I have to get out of here before she does.* I didn't realize how frightened he was of being abandoned again, by yet another woman.

24.
PSYCH EVALUATIONS: SEPTEMBER 2017

"There's some undetermined pathology with him, I can't put my finger on it," my mom would say. "He needs to stop doing everything for everybody and then resenting them for it."

I didn't put much weight in her armchair diagnosis; remember, she's the one who told me I had Hysterical Personality Disorder. She also said, given my history with men, that my boyfriends had "gotten progressively worse" over the years. On that one, I had to admit she was right.

We'd tried so many marriage counselors but none of them were able to help us. Fabio remained cool, calm, and collected during the sessions, reticent to share honestly. He would sit there quietly, eyes to the ground, and softly say, "But I love her. I only want to make her happy." They never met the dissociative, raging monster who lived with me or fell victim to his constant verbal trickery. Once again, this was all going to fall on my shoulders to fix. I researched online for anything that could help and stumbled upon "Grown Wounded Child," an online course written by Peter K. Gerlach, MSW. *This is the answer! He's a loner, he doesn't like to share intimately. Maybe he can fix himself!*

I reviewed the questions Dr. Gerlach used to determine if you were a Grown Wounded Child and it seemed to me that Fabio had at least 31 of the 40 determining factors. He agreed to give it a try, took the test, but would only admit to 15. When I asked him to take it again, but be brutally honest with himself, he agreed to the 20 required to qualify and set about doing the self-work. I was hopeful it would help him recognize how his avoidance and dismissiveness were hurting our marriage. Fabio had always told me that his cruelty toward me was due to the stress we'd both been living under and that he would be happy and relaxed once we got to Panama, but I wasn't so sure.

He never completed the course and we were back to square one.

Things were escalating pretty quickly in the summer of 2017. We were selling everything in preparation to move to our island retirement home. I suggested we try another round of counseling before we moved away, this time with an older, male therapist I thought would feel more like a father figure to Fabio. The majority of our previous therapists had been women whom he was able to charm. During our third session with him, the doctor announced, "Something doesn't add up here; let's do psychological testing."

We each took the test, 200 or so questions, and scheduled our individual follow-ups with the doctor. We received the results and Fabio's was absolutely terrifying… sociopathic, with all the signs of a covert narcissist, and sadistic. Finally, everything made sense to me; that's who I saw at home, not the mask he wore for others. I asked him what he thought of his report and he replied, "That's me, 100%." *I knew it, I knew it all along.* I just needed confirmation in writing to believe that my husband was, in fact, a monster.

You be careful. People in masks cannot be trusted.

When I read this paragraph from his psych report I stopped breathing and froze completely solid. I would never feel safe alone with him in Panama…

Most notable is his overtly rough or pugnacious temper, which periodically flares into contentious arguments or physical belligerence, the latter evident occasionally in a fractious willingness to harm others. Beyond his callous disdain for the rights of others, he may be deficient in the capacity to share tender feelings, to experience genuine affection and love, or to empathize with others' needs. If he has extremely vicious tendencies, he may experience a deep sense of pleasure at the mere thought of hurting others or seeing them downtrodden and suffering.

The following words jumped off the page at me, words to describe my husband's personality:

Anxiety
Borderline
Cognitively Fatalistic
Delusional Disorder
Dependent (17 occurrences)
Depressive
Fatalistic
Major Thought Disorder
Sadistic
Suicidal
Temperamentally Hostile

In my private follow-up meeting with the therapist, he looked me squarely in the eye and said, "I would not go to Panama if I were you, he could kill you in a dissociative rage," and I knew it was true and that I may never survive if I went. I could end up murdered, cut into tiny pieces, and tossed into the jungle to rot, or maybe thrown overboard. I imagined the story he would tell everyone. "We had a fight and she left. I haven't heard from her and don't know where she is," delivered sans emotion. At the conclusion of our follow-up meeting, the therapist asked me, "Have you spoken to the first wife?" More on that later.

My psych report revealed what I had already come to know about myself. The two most notable scores were histrionic[53] and compulsion. Histrionics crave attention and seek reassurance and approval from external sources. That made perfect sense to me, for a person who grew up receiving so little love and attention from her own parents. But because I don't wear makeup, or heels, or dress with my tatas hanging out, I'm confident my histrionic tendencies are not at a disordered level. Histrionics are also quite gullible and easily influenced by others. I was primed from a very young age to become codependent and at risk of being taken advantage of by a love bombing predator.

My tendency toward compulsion is how I control my out-of-control surroundings. I need to have order in my world and I seek to create it for myself. It gives me a sense of stability and helps me to feel safe. My compulsive traits have served me well both in life and in business. I never lose my keys and never forget an appointment.

____

[53] "Histrionic" • A person with histrionic personality disorder seeks attention, talks dramatically with strong opinions, is easily influenced, has rapidly changing emotions, and thinks relationships are closer than they are.

25.
HEALTH SIDE EFFECTS, BOTH MENTAL AND PHYSICAL

Living under any kind of chronic stress is bad for your health, but living with a narcissist could actually kill you. The insidious ways they devalue you day after day take a toll on your mind and in your body. The narcissist's inherent toxicity, just like a spider's, paralyzes you, making it difficult to escape.

I could no longer read. New skills and other people's ideas delivered by the written word were beyond my ability to comprehend. I listened to the same, familiar music over and over again; it was the only thing that comforted me, yet I didn't understand why. For a girl that had spent her entire career listening to brand-new bands and choosing hit songs from unknown artists to share with the rest of the world, it was a huge loss to my tender soul. Music had always been my drug of choice and I didn't even enjoy listening to new records anymore.

During the early '00s, Radiohead's catalog remained in my car's multidisc CD player for several years, spinning over and over and over again. Fabio teased me for it, and of course, he hated Radiohead. He'd suddenly grown to hate everything I loved. The only way I could understand any new concept was to have it explained to me verbally, and only while I was performing the actual task. Reading news stories online became virtually impossible. I might be able to get through the headline, and perhaps a sentence or two, only to have to go back to the beginning and reread it all over again for comprehension. Eventually, I would give up, mid-article, and hope no one wanted to discuss world events.

I thought I was going nuts; reading used to bring me so much joy. If you ever looked in my handbag you would always find a novel at the bottom. It used to relax me, but now it only stressed me out. I kept this shame to myself for a very long time. Every now and again a friend would loan me a book they recommended, remembering that I'd once been a voracious reader. I would try to get through it, only to give up in tears and wonder why I could no longer focus my attention.

"How did you like it?"

"Oh, it was great, thanks for lending it to me, gotta run."

I couldn't even follow an hour-long drama on TV, or sit in the same room with him during an action movie. I'd have to leave and hide in the upstairs bedroom listening to yoga music while doing my breathing exercises. I was jumpy all the time.

I attributed it to all the stress I was experiencing from trying to please the customers at my music school and Fabio reinforced that belief. I'd also been smoking pot on a daily basis for the past few years to cope, and I knew I couldn't give up marijuana and stay with him.

Chronic back pain from a serious car accident that occurred in 2002 plagued me. I'd lie on the cold, hard linoleum floor of our den to watch TV because I could no longer sit in a chair. The pain was excruciating; I wore heated back pads day and night. The injury wouldn't heal because I was under constant stress, but Fabio kept telling me I was making it up to avoid being on top during sex.

Once he left for Panama for good, and after living for 20 years in constant pain, I finally found a chiropractor who determined that I'd been walking around with my right leg half an inch shorter than my left leg for all that time. Years of built-up scar tissue needed to be broken down but now, without the daily stress of a manipulator in charge of my every move, I've finally healed.

The most debilitating part of it all was that I couldn't sleep for more than two hours at a time – he hit me in the middle of the night, by accident he said, but I'd shared a bed with my first husband and was never hit in the middle of the night, not once. He snored but refused to admit it. "You're making that up!" he would scream. Julian would confirm that he had to get up in the middle of the night to close both his door and ours. To Julian: "You're making that up too!" I should have recorded him.

He was restless in bed, rolling back and forth and back and forth. Guilty conscience? When he woke up before me he would leap out of bed and turn all the lights on, waking me up too. "*Pleease* Fabio," I groaned as I pulled a pillow over my eyes. Eye roll, harrumph – no change. I ended up addicted to Xanax and eventually, after two inconclusive sleep studies, was prescribed Xyrem to sleep, a date rape drug.

After 10 years of trying to share a bed with him, I asked him to move to the second master suite of our house and I'm going to guess that was the day the online girlfriends and nightly porn began. There was a reason he'd set his browsers up to not track any of his activity, and why when I would ask him what he'd been up to while I was at work, the answer was always, "Nothing."

A couple of times, when we were walking the dog together around the Mountain, the stress I was feeling overwhelmed me and I would confess to him, "I'm so unhappy Fabio, I want to die." And guess what he said? Nothing; although I could imagine inside he was thinking, "Ha, ha, my work is almost done here." Evil to the core; he hated me and I didn't even realize it as it was happening.

Living with chronic anxiety is the absolute worst thing you can do for your long-term health. Taking toxic prescription medicines for sleep will destroy your natural sleep architecture and after a year or so of taking them, they no longer work anyway. I was grinding my teeth at night and eventually had to have six of them pulled and replaced with implants. A patch of eczema formed on my lower back that wouldn't go away.

But the worst thing of all happened in 2005, the year after we became husband and wife. One Saturday morning I woke up and nothing seemed wrong until I went into the bathroom to brush my teeth. I looked up in the mirror and the entire left side of my face had fallen; I looked like a Salvador Dali painting. I screamed and heard a nonchalant, "What's up?" coming from the second-floor office. I ran downstairs crying. "Look at me! What's happened? Did I have a stroke? Fabio, I'm scared." There was no response at all from him, no verbal reassurance or supportive statements. He just began calmly researching on the Internet to see what had happened. "I think you have Bell's Palsy,[54] probably from a deer tick with Lyme disease."

We rushed to the hospital and they confirmed it. I was given an antibiotic but it wasn't strong enough and I was eventually admitted. At my bedside, three doctors argued over my treatment until two won out and I was administered the strongest broad-spectrum antibiotic

---

[54] "Bell's Palsy" • Paralysis of the facial nerve causing muscular weakness in one side of the face.

they could give me. A PICC line[55] was inserted into my arm that delivered Rocephin, 24 hours a day, directly into my heart. I carried a pole with a drip bag for the next three weeks. Fabio's only response to my illness was to ask if I would like to attend the Live 8 concert on the Benjamin Franklin Parkway that weekend, to see Beyoncé and JayZ. He thought it would cheer me up.

"Why would I want to do that? With a patch over my left eye and dragging a drip pole through a crowd of 800,000 people in this heat? What if anyone I knew saw me like that?" but he was insensitive to my pain or maybe he knew exactly what he was saying and he was just a monster, without empathy. "Fabio, if I got cancer you wouldn't stick around for me, would you?" No response from him ever, because he knew it was true.

My Bell's Palsy never fully healed as a result of taking drugs to sleep. Benzodiazepines prevent stages 3 and 4 restorative sleep; I never knew that.

It was another sign from the Universe to get out and get out now, but my hardwired brain was stronger than my cognitive ability, and I kept thinking it would get better now that we were married.

Precancerous lesions called actinic keratosis formed all over my forehead and I thought I may only be able to

---

[55] "PICC line" • A long catheter that is inserted through a peripheral vein, often in the arm, into a larger vein in the body, used when intravenous treatment is required over a long period.

enjoy Panama life before the sun rose or at night, after it set. I didn't put it all together because it was one thing after the next. My body was breaking down from chronic stress and I was afraid I'd develop a systemic disease.

26.

THEFT OF $100,000 PRENUP: SEPTEMBER 2017

As you know, when we first met back in 1999 I lived in a cute little section of Philadelphia called Manayunk. I loved the energy there and my sweet little house even more. I only paid $53,000 for it but it was the prettiest house in town with a big backyard for a vegetable garden and a massive clawfoot soaking tub upstairs. It was my sanctuary after marriage #1 hit the skids.

When Fabio convinced me to sell my beloved home so we could move in together, I did so reluctantly. It broke my heart to give up my little home but there was no way I could afford to keep it and move into the new school district I thought best for Julian. Layla was in 8th grade at the time and I did not want to disrupt a young teen like my parents had done to me when I was her age.

You recall, Fabio had no money to put down on the Valley Forge house, blaming his first wife for spending all his money, but he did have a good-paying job, so I put in $100,000 as a down payment but not without protection. We both signed an agreement which we then had notarized, acknowledging my $100,000 down payment and stating that I would receive the first $100,000 of proceeds from the sale of the home if we ever sold the house or split up.

We received an offer on the Valley Forge house in September of 2017 so I checked my files for the agreement and it was missing. I asked Fabio if he knew what happened to it and he launched into what seemed to be a prepared story. I'd ripped it up, he said. I must have forgotten. Maybe I have a brain tumor. Maybe I'm going crazy. He'd tried to get me to write a new agreement to cancel it but I said he was overthinking things and ripped it up right in front of him. He just can't believe I don't remember ripping it up and forgiving him the money four years prior because he'd cosigned a lease for Rock & Roll After School.

As if anyone would forget ripping up a $100,000 agreement only four years prior, anyone. I bet he stole it when I threatened to go on a "date," and he moved to the condo where I kept my files.

He stole my $100,000 prenup and tried to gaslight me about it. Yes, he did, and I have a written email from him with his made-up story to prove it.

27.

ABANDONED IN LANCASTER: JANUARY 2018

We were wrapping up all our final responsibilities in preparation to move to Panama… sell Rock & Roll After School and train the new owners; sell the house; move my mom to assisted living; and prepare the apartment unit in the Lancaster property for rent. Today was Lancaster.

We drove our Ford Transit Connect to Julian's with a list of "to-dos." Fabio focused on the long, straight drive down Route 30 but something in the air felt eerie that day; I couldn't put my finger on it. I could tell he was mad about something, so I did what I always do – stayed out of his space and kept silent the entire trip.

On my list was some light yard work and staging the apartment unit in the front. I asked Fabio if he could gather all of the bunk bed parts together from the upstairs bedroom, the side guardrails from the attic, and the joining pins from the drawer in the front room, and assemble the beds. That way, we could easily donate it to one of the families living in the projects across the street.

We arrived at Julian's and I immediately went to the back of the house to get away from Fabio's angry vibe and let him put the beds together on his own. After about 30 minutes of banging and grunting sounds, Fabio came to the kitchen holding two side guardrails from the top bunk saying, "These boards aren't needed, I'm putting them back in the attic." I knew to choose my words carefully, so I asked, "Can you show me why they aren't needed?" and followed him to the apartment unit, looked at the beds pushed up against the wall, and repeated, "I really wanted to have all of the parts together so I can donate it when we no longer need it."

Before I knew it, Fabio was in a full-blown, volcanic rage. I couldn't even process the insults and accusations being hurled at me. Then, he stormed out the front door screaming, "I never want to see your face again," and slammed the door shut. Less than 10 seconds later he began to push the door back in and I defiantly said, "Well, you'd better not open that door, because my FACE is on the other side of it."

I heard him drive away. He left me in Lancaster without any money, no phone charger, no blankets or sheets to sleep on, and a knot in my stomach as big as a basketball.

After working on the house, we had plans to dine with the Tarsias, and Fabio or no Fabio, I was not going to let him ruin my night so I called my buddy Joe and asked him to swing by and pick me up. The three of us had a simply lovely evening, where his wife Cecelia went on and on like a fangirl to all the waiters or anyone who would listen, about her amazing husband Joe, the world-famous recording engineer, while I wondered to myself why I couldn't have an amazing husband who loved me.

When I returned to the house after dinner, I called my trusty, lifelong friend Dar who listened to the whole story and called my ex, Tom, knowing that he would be able to make me laugh, and he did. I hadn't spoken to Tom in five years. Fabio made it impossible for me to have male friends. I didn't care what he thought anymore. *I will be friends with whomever I want to be!*

I stayed awake all night and at 6:30 a.m., called Fabio to ask when he would be picking me up. He replied, "Why can't Julian bring you home?"

"He has to work and he didn't abandon me here, you did."

The 90-minute ride home together felt like two eternities; Fabio would not look at me or respond to anything I asked him. He pulled up to our condo building, dropped me off, and sped away. When I walked inside I saw that he'd stayed awake all night, completely ransacked the place, and every single item of his was gone. What he left behind was symbolic… his wedding suit hanging in the closet, Birkenstock sandals on the floor beneath it, the "Dude" sweater I gave him as a gift, and three pieces of his first wife Laura's furniture. He took every coffee cup, sock, and paper clip he felt was his (and really, anything else he wanted).

I still wasn't ready to give up. I'd invested so many years in him and so much was riding on the line. The Sunk Cost Fallacy[56] was operating in full swing.

------

[56] "Sunk Cost Fallacy" • Our tendency to follow through on an endeavor in which we've already invested time, effort, or money, even if the costs outweigh the benefits.

28.
13-HOUR FIGHT #2 –
PANAMA HOUSE:
FEBRUARY 2018

Where it started...

We took our final trip to Panama together in early February 2018. We had just notified the Rock & Roll After School staff that the school had been sold and the new owners would be taking over the following month. We were excited to be finalizing the details to make our permanent move to the retirement home we'd been building for nearly seven years. I put all my fears and negative thoughts away and focused on the positive. I'm *so* good at that!

We enjoyed a romantic dinner at our favorite restaurant, Caliope, and meandered through the cobblestone streets holding hands. On Monday morning we visited the Immigration office and Fabio turned in our company stock certificates. My dream of retiring at the beach was becoming a reality.

The next night, while relaxing in our Casco Viejo hotel, I heard Fabio utter a groan. "What's up?" He showed me his computer and I started to read. Layla had emailed him a contract she'd written, whereby she would agree to reach out to me one last time before we moved. *A contract? Where did she learn to do that? Hmm, I'm guessing her dad.*

I was shocked and saddened that it had come to this. Fabio said she was crazy. Years later, I reread her words and have come to realize that she is not crazy at all. She may be the smartest and most intuitive member of the family. He tried to cripple her emotionally, to make her dependent on him for life, but she wasn't fooled by his words any longer and clearly didn't trust him. She'd been out of the house for several years by now and had the time alone to reflect on everything she'd been through.

We flew from Panama City to Bocas that Thursday on the tiny commuter plane that flies there two times per day. The plane landed at the airport in Bocas Town adjacent to the local neighborhood, La Solución, with the high school baseball field awkwardly positioned at the end of the runway. You would frequently see kids moving to the edge of the fence to allow the planes to come in, then resume playing ball once they'd landed.

We bought a hammock for the front deck from a local street vendor and hailed a cab that took us the rough and muddy eight miles, all the way up Blave Beach Road to our nearly-completed new home. We were both exhausted but the furniture was still in Philly so we inflated the mattress we bought at Costco that we would sleep on until our builders finished the platform bed I'd designed for us.

The next morning, we were standing next to each other on the upstairs deck that overlooked the Caribbean, a place I'd assumed we would finally find our peace and live happily ever after.

We were discussing where to hang the hammock. I looked up to the tops of the natural wood trees I'd chosen to support the roof overhang and identified an area where we could secure the hammock between the top of the middle pillar and the one on the right front corner of the deck. I said, "Hey Fabio, I know where we can hang the hammock," and proceeded to point out what I had noticed. I assumed he was listening to me while he kept his gaze focused on the top of the center pole, but I should have known better. He heard what I said but as soon as I finished speaking replied, "I know where we can secure the hammock, right there, at the top of the center pole, and extend it on an angle to the front right pole." *Huh? Isn't that what I just said?*

As usual, his reply was that he didn't hear it or that maybe I just thought it but didn't say it. I later learned that this was all done on purpose to show me that nothing would be different in Panama. I felt a chill come over my entire body but pushed down the uncomfortable feeling and proceeded inside, to the closet. "Fabio, I don't want a single closet bar that extends the length of the closet. I would prefer two bars on the right side to hang shirts and skirts and one bar on the left for sundresses and cover-ups. Maybe some cubbies in the middle for sandals and swim fins." He slowly walked over to the closet door, looked left and then right, and said, "So you want a single bar that goes from one end to the other, right? No shelves, no cubbies for shoes?"

Infuriating and obviously intentional; I just hadn't fully realized the extent of his plan to discard and replace me.

How it ended...

I went absolutely nuts, "Why do you do this to me? I know you heard me." Fabio made his way to the edge of the deck, took his wedding ring off, and threw it over the railing. I didn't know at the time he'd only pretended to. His reactions to my expressed frustrations were always overly dramatic, right from the very early days of our relationship when he would strip the walls of all of Layla's photos.

I can't remember anything that happened from the beginning of that argument in the closet until the very end at 4 a.m. when I stated in complete frustration, "When I get home, I'm going to blow David Fagin," whom I hadn't even spoken to for the past 15 years. No matter how many times he'd baited me, I'd only once before snapped like that and said something I knew to be completely untrue when I threatened to go on a "date." I just couldn't figure out any other way to stop him before the sun came up. Dejectedly, I climbed up the stairs to lie awake on the air mattress and he fell asleep on the hardwood floor downstairs in the bedroom.

He had promised me he would never act that way in Bocas but that was a lie. He started this fight intentionally to instill fear in me about moving to Panama with him so he could complete his master plan to discard me and move on with as many of our assets as he could possibly get his hands on.

29.
LEAVING FOR BOCAS: MARCH 2018

The stress we were both under was crippling and our marriage was breaking at the seams. He picked fight after fight leading up to the day he'd planned to drive to Florida in the U-Haul packed with our furniture and personal belongings for transport to Bocas del Toro. I pleaded with him to include me in his plans but he stonewalled me again and again. Fabio was always leaving in the middle of arguments to stay at either the school or the Valley Forge house, and once that house was sold, he would drive an hour and 30 minutes to Lancaster to sleep in Julian's extra room rather than stay and work it out with me. I told him I thought he suffered from Avoidant Attachment Disorder, but his narcissistic behaviors were pervasive, and the damage that had been inflicted on him as a young boy went much deeper.

"There are 10 divorces among your five siblings," I shouted at him. "What the hell is that? That's got to be some kind of record."

"Yeah, well us Vendittis are superior in every way," he boasted, wearing a devilish grin, "even divorces!" There was no end to his arrogance. Brother Milo had been divorced so many times that Fabio refused to learn the fifth one's name. "Cinco," he called her, "Cinco de Milo," but suddenly Milo was his new hero. "He's simply a romantic, eternally hopeful, and what impresses me the most about him is that he always has one waiting in the wings." That was his way of letting me know that he too had one "waiting in the wings," while laughing at me internally as it passed straight over my head. It wasn't until after it was all over that I thought back over his many veiled "confessions." He knew he was a narcissist, and rather proud of his covert style.

He accused me of cheating with my ex-boyfriend when it was he who was the cheater all along.

Him: I bet you're in touch with Tom behind my back.

Me: Nope, I said calmly, haven't talked to him in over five years, just like you asked.

Him: Then you're in touch with him over Facebook.

Me: Okay buddy, let's go look at my messages together.

Him: You probably deleted it.

Me: You're baiting me, Fabio! Admit it.

I said it with newfound confidence. No response from

him; he knew it was true and he needed to get out fast before I figured out he'd already decided a long time ago he was going to Bocas without me. I held the phone up, "Fine then, let's call him now. Say his name one more time and I'm dialing." He finally gave up, backed into a corner of his own lies. Projection is the narcissist's playbook. Whatever they are accusing you of is what they are doing themselves.

"Your penis is a bigger problem for you than it is for me and I am not a cheater. Cheaters are liars and I am neither of those things." He had no response to this either because he knew I was telling the truth. "If you're unhappy with me, go get yourself a girlfriend who wants this shit because I don't want it." Little did I know…

"Deal with your shit," I said, "although I know you never will." I was desperate to reach him; I just didn't know how. "You hide away from everyone pretending to be someone you're not. You have become Spock, mixed with Kwai Chang Caine, and pretend you have real connections with people but no one really knows you. Not even your own family!"

I screamed at him, "You are The Overlord, The Punisher, a Demon. You are not a husband! You are a Dark Force!" I remembered back to 20 years ago when Dar called him "joyless." Why hadn't I listened to her? I was losing control of myself, spinning down the vortex of the drain that our marriage had become.

I came out to find him in the living room checking my phone every day, pretending to be updating the software for me. I caught him multiple times and challenged him. "You've been checking my phone every day for 19 years now. Ever find anything?"

"No," he cried.

"Ever going to stop?"

"*Nooo*," while crying his crocodile tears at me. He could turn those tears on and off at will.

He hacked my email and made up stories about what he imagined he'd read there. The accusations were flying now. He screamed at me, "All your friends hate you!"

"Really? They must hate themselves too, otherwise, why do they want to hang with me?"

"You're losing your punching bag," I declared.

"Yeah, well what about what you did," blame-shifting[57] me again.

"We can talk all day and night about what I did once you've answered my fucking question." He was yelling at me so loudly in our King of Prussia condo, I was afraid

____

[57] "Blame-Shifting" • Blame-shifting is a manipulation technique that narcissists and other emotionally abusive controlling people will use to distract attention from their behavior and shift the responsibility for any errors to someone else.

the neighbors would hear us through the walls and call the police.

The tricks were flying fast and furious now. He was determined to keep me confused until he had all his ducks lined up. "How come you're not friends with any of your exes?" I screamed at him.

"I don't have as many as you."

Word salad is used intentionally by a malignant narcissist to manipulate others, so that you question yourself, rather than question them. Once I realized his behavior was intentional, he'd finally met his match. The survival brain I'd relied on since childhood made me unassailable.

Me: You don't understand anything I say!

Him: I understand EVERYTHING you say!

Me: Then it IS intentional.

Still confused, but fighting back with everything I had. *Maybe if I call Evelyn, she knows who he is, maybe she can talk to him.* I dialed her number. "Mom, your son needs you, he's in real trouble. We've been fighting and living apart for almost a year now and I just can't fix this by myself. He has no real friends, no one he can confide in, please talk to him, please. I'm begging you, help your son!" I guess I shouldn't have been surprised by her response but all she said was, "Why don't you ever call me anymore? You used to call me, but now I rarely hear from you." *What? How did she just turn this around to be about her? Her son needs her.*

Things became a lot clearer to me in that moment. Fabio learned these avoidance and deflection tactics from his mother. I tried to answer her, "Mom, I don't feel comfortable calling you ever since you told Fabio to divorce me and kick me to the curb back when Layla graduated college." Her response: "I never said that," completely denying it. My mind was spinning, I couldn't tell up from down, so I handed the phone to Fabio and walked into the bedroom to cry tears of frustration.

Ever since the Catholic ceremony, I was no longer falling for his tricks. I was proud of myself. I'd had enough and decided not to go to Bocas with him until October, after he'd had a chance to calm down, to be alone for a while, reflect on his actions, and hopefully, miss me.

Eventually, the apologies started to flow, the best he could give me, all delivered while shrieking at me and running in the opposite direction, "I'm sorry I made you wait all those times," finally admitting that the home projects had been dragged out intentionally, and "I'm sorry I made you silent in bed."

I no longer trusted him. I knew if I went to Bocas I'd be isolated from my friends and family. He could kill me in a fit of rage. I could see clearly now and the image of him dropping a knife into my chest was vivid in my mind.

I had grown my hair out for four years in preparation to tie it back on our eventual boat. We'd dreamed of sailing the Caribbean together; he even took sailing lessons on the Delaware Riverfront. We'd named all of our future chickens – Parmigiana, Cacciatore, Piccata, Marsala, General Tso, Kung Pao, Paprikash... you get the idea. The baby chicks would all be called Nugget, and we would name the teens, Tender. We laughed together, sharing dreams of our happy future. I had to come to the realization that none of it was ever true and my plans to become a permaculture chef living at the beach were permanently dashed.

This is what's known as future faking[58] and narcissists use this tactic to set you up so they can steal whatever they can from you before they move on to their next target.

---

[58] "Future Faking" • When someone uses a detailed vision of the future to facilitate bonding and connection in a romantic relationship. A narcissist's staple.

30.
THE FLYING MONKEYS[59]

One by one, my friends began calling me with concern.

"How are you doing, Erin? Are you okay?"

"Sure, I'm fine. Why are you asking me that?"

"Hmm, no reason, just making sure you're okay."

These calls seemed to be coming out of the blue and when I wasn't satisfied with their responses, I repeated… "I'm asking you, why are you asking me that?"

"Well… Fabio called me yesterday and he told me some very frightening things."

"What did he say?"

"I won't tell you; that's between him and me but it's all fine, we're good. I'm no longer concerned now that we've spoken."

---

[59] "Flying Monkeys" • Flying monkeys are people who actively participate in a narcissist's smear campaign. The goal of the campaign is to destroy the target's reputation.

I eventually learned he was telling everyone that he was afraid I was going to harm myself when nothing could've been farther from the truth.

He attended a local music show alone one night, something he'd never done before. Local pop heroes, "The Cliff Hillis Moment," were performing at Steel City Coffeehouse and my best friend Elise, and her husband Patrick were going to be there.

"I think Erin has changed her mind about going to Bocas," he confided in her.

Elise responded with, "No, I don't think so," but still, it created a tiny sense of doubt, and that was his goal.

His family all unfriended my son and me on the same day. What had he told them? I will never know because of the Venditti family motto. "If you're not at lunch, you ARE lunch." It's like *The Sopranos* over there in Venditti Land.

I doubled down; I didn't want to let go. I'd worked all my life for my retirement at the beach and could feel it slipping away from me. I cried to Dar.

"But he's handsome and sexy, he's smart and talented, he can fix things, sometimes he's fun, and always helpful."

"Stop reading me that list in your head of his good qualities," she barked back at me. "You're trying to convince yourself he's alright. He is NOT alright."

Dar is a sage. She is the only one in my circle of friends to try and warn me about both of my husbands.

Driving down Route 422 in hysterical tears I cried to myself, "Who could I tell and where would I start?" I was on my way to my monthly sushi date with Michelle and decided to take a chance. I told her everything. "I didn't realize how bad it had become," she said to me in the parking lot after dinner. "I'm so sorry, Erin." There, it was finally out. I felt a sigh of relief knowing I had someone I could talk to.

31.
DISCARD AND DIVORCE: APRIL 2017–JULY 2019

I'm not sure when it started but he began bringing me coffee every morning, perfectly prepared, just how I like it. He'd never done that before, not in 20 years together, and I did think that something was up, although I wasn't sure what it was. Was he turning over a new leaf in preparation for us to retire together in Panama? He would smile at me as he handed me the mug in our upstairs office. I would cock my head and wonder, *where's this coming from?* But simply say, "Thank you, Fabio," and go back to my work. Something was amiss. I could feel it.

I'll never know exactly when he made his final decision to go to Panama without me but ever since Layla's Catholic ceremony, and most likely long before that, he'd been carefully stacking the cards in his favor in the event he needed to discard me and go alone. His tricks no longer worked on me and he'd confessed his darkest secrets on the carpet of our master bedroom during the 13-hour talk we had back in May of 2017. The false self had been cracked wide open and the scared little boy underneath was on full display.

Narcissists fear vulnerability and will do anything to protect their fragile egos. Sadly, for both of us, all I ever wanted was his vulnerability. I wanted him to trust me, to share his life with me, to treat me like a true partner. I never once betrayed him but it wasn't enough to erase what his mom and those girls had done to him when he was so young and impressionable. He'd made a conscious decision to shut down, to be emotionless so no one could hurt him or get close to him. No one ever, not even after 20 years of trying.

The storage locker we'd rented was filled with the contents of our Valley Forge home, packed up, and ready to move to Bocas. Stuffed to the gills with all of my worldly possessions, including my family's antiques, wall hangings and décor, kitchen gadgets I'd purchased for our permaculture homestead, my summer clothes, beloved sea glass collection, broken jewelry to mosaic the house with, and his tools from our garage.

I begged him to talk with me but all he said was that he wanted to time it out so he didn't have to spend more than three days staying with his mother in Florida. The problem was we weren't exactly sure what day the container was leaving so the timing was unsure. "Please Fabio, talk with me." Nope; he'd already decided he was going alone but wasn't going to tell me.

He picked up the U-Haul truck on Monday, drove it over to the storage locker to pack it up, and returned to the condo to grab his suitcase. I followed him down to the parking lot and watched him unlatch the rear door and roll it up, revealing all my things carefully stacked inside. Then, I noticed something in the back corner. "Why are you taking the Christmas ornaments? I thought we'd be spending the holidays in the States with my family like we always do." Clearly, I am in complete denial of what is happening right before my very eyes.

"I'm going to Bocas and I'm NEVER coming back here again," he growled at me between his teeth, his eyes blackened with anger. I was terrified of him. Then he jumped into the truck and drove away, leaving me standing there alone in the parking lot, bawling my eyes out. *There goes your entire life Erin, and your dream of living at the beach, gone forever.*

The Catholic ceremony argument, the frightening psych report, my mom moved into a nursing home… we'd sold our house, our business, followed by his abandonment of me at Julian's home in Lancaster while stripping our condo of every single one of his possessions in the middle of the night, the constant threats and accusations of cheating, the parking lot rage as he pulled away in a U-Haul truck filled with everything I'd ever owned, and soon he'd be moving my beloved Bernese Mountain dog/daughter Calle, whom I would never see again.

This all happened within a mere 12 months' time span. They say don't make any important decisions after just one of these life-altering events but Fabio was the decider and he'd already made his decision to leave me; he just neglected to tell me first. The signs were there but my survival brain would not allow me to see them.

After he left, I reconnected with David Fagin after 15 years. I emailed him.

"Surprise! I know you're coming to Philly for a wedding gig. Can we have lunch?"

"Of course, Erin. It's great to hear from you."

Real friends forgive you and listen to what you have to say. We sat down at the table and I started the conversation. "I'm sorry I've been gone from you all these years. It wasn't me, it was Fabio. He made it impossible for me to stay friends with you, constantly accusing me of wanting to sleep with you. It was simply unbearable, so I had to pull away." David joked, "Well then, I guess we should have slept together, haha, if you're going to be accused of it anyway!" Too funny! We both laughed out loud. What an ice breaker; I'd missed his quick sense of humor and it felt good to laugh again. I was taking my power back and Fabio was not going to decide who I was allowed to be friends with ever again.

Next stop, repairing things with Tom. I'd been pretty cruel to him to push him away. There was no other way for me to get rid of him without being mean; I'd loved him for too long. Just like David, he forgave me immediately. Tom has turned out to be one of the most meaningful and healing friendships of my entire life. We met when I was only 24 years old, dated from 26 to 30, and have been the closest of friends ever since. Thirty-nine years of true friendship (minus the five I wasn't allowed to) is a testament to the fact that you can retain closeness with an ex and have it grow into a lifelong connection. As you know from Chapter 1, friends have been my stable rock throughout my life and I am grateful for the wonderful people I know and love, and who love me right back.

In early April, Fabio forwarded me a Temporary Separation Agreement that he wrote himself. He said it was to "protect me" in the event something happened to him while we were living apart and so I could qualify for health insurance through the ACA[60] website.

The precancerous lesions on my forehead were showing signs of turning malignant and I needed to see a dermatologist right away. Fabio had gotten himself health insurance the minute he arrived in Panama but I was left without.

"I'm just looking out for you, Erin. What if I died of a heart attack? The condo in the States would go into probate and you know you and Layla don't get along. She'd make a claim to it, you'd have to sell it and split the proceeds with her," triangulating me against her, but this time from a distance.

---

[60] "Affordable Care Act" • A landmark U.S. federal statute making health insurance available to more Americans, enacted by the 111th United States Congress and signed into law by President Barack Obama on March 23, 2010.

I was vulnerable and scared at the time and would have signed anything. I took the agreement to a lawyer, albeit a bad one, and resigned myself to the idea that I had no other choice but to sign whatever I was given. Fabio refused all of the negotiating points my lawyer suggested. I feared he would steal everything and I'd end up homeless, homeless with cancer. Unbeknownst to me, I'd been tricked into signing a temporary agreement that he could roll into something permanent. I wanted to believe him with all my heart that he couldn't, wouldn't, after 20 years, hurt me like that, but I was dead wrong.

He had me go to Costco to get him a lifetime supply of prescription contacts and asked me to rip our DVD collection to an external hard drive and ship it to him. One by one I transferred over 100 movies, a two-week all-day-all-night project, so he could have movies to watch in Panama. What a fool I was, blindly loyal until the bitter end, but deep within my soul, I could feel his lies. I didn't trust him anymore while still telling myself the time apart would fix things.

He's happier now that he's in Bocas. That's what he said. He hasn't cussed or yelled once while working on the house. He fixed a little boy's bike that had broken down along the road. He could feel himself coming back to life and couldn't wait to share his true self with me, the one and only love of his life.

"I love you and I still have faith in us. I wish you were here, nothing's as good without you," he emailed me, along with a photo of a cold beer from our favorite outdoor drinking hole, La Rana Dorada. "I love you more than I will ever be able to explain and more than you will ever believe or trust. I'm especially sorry for that – making you not trust or believe me."

"Which way do you want me to lay the bedroom tile, honey?" And the next day… "We have Internet," he proclaimed, sending me a photo of the satellite dish attached to the corner of the roof. *Who is this WE you're talking about?* I couldn't even respond. I lay dying inside because I knew I would never see any of it.

He drew hearts in the sand with our initials on the beach in front of our Bocas home.

"You are the love of my life, Erin. I can't wait until you get here and we can begin our new life together." At the same time he was already online grooming his next source of supply.

Hoovering[61] is what they call it when a narcissist tries to draw you back in, like a vacuum cleaner, just before the final discard.

In late April 2018, he planned to return to Philadelphia, pick up the dog, and transport her to Panama.

----

[61] "Hoovering" • Like the famous Hoover vacuum cleaner, the narcissist sucks you back into their lives, usually after a breakup, discard, or your leaving the relationship. It will typically begin slowly and appear well intended.

From: Fabio
To: Erin
Subject: Tomorrow and Onward
Date: April 27, 2018 at 10:41:38 PM EDT

I imagine you are as nervous and unsure about the next few days as I am.
My goal is simple.
Love
I will talk about whatever you need to.
I will do my best to not appear avoidant or dismissive.
Above all I hope to show you, in all my behavior, the love I feel for you.

He asked if I would allow him to stay with me in the condo, or would I prefer he stay in a hotel? I desperately wanted to work things out so I said, "Condo, of course." During the two weeks he was home, he escalated his war against me to a frightening level. Daily accusations of cheating on him with Tom and David were hurled at me, but he offered no proof. So much for "the love I feel for you." I tried to reassure him I was completely loyal and dedicated to our marriage… full speed ahead to our dream retirement together.

To prove my loyalty, I offered to take him to New York City to see our friend Dan Reed with his band, The Network. After the show, we would go see David's band perform at a nearby charity event. I wanted him to see for himself that David and I were friends; we'd always been just friends. I simply wanted to be trusted and allowed to choose my own friends. David's girlfriend of

20+ years, Paula, was going to be there too; that HAD to reassure him. He agreed to go. Before Dan's show at the Iridium nightclub, we enjoyed a nice Italian dinner at Monte's Trattoria in the West Village and I checked us in on Facebook… "Dining with My Love." He seemed touched by my post. I was still trying to fix things. After the show, I asked him to come with me over to David's show. No fucking way. He knew the truth, but it didn't fit in with his plans to discard me, so we hopped the train home.

It was becoming more and more clear that he didn't care one bit about me, yet I doubled down in denial. He'd purchased an open-air four-wheel-drive quad while in Panama. I had asked him if we could please buy a golf cart with a roof, to protect me from getting skin cancer, but he already knew I wasn't coming.

It took a few tries and trips to and from the airport to get the right-sized crate and a flight that would take Calle to Panama. Three failed attempts out of Philly, and he decided to drive to Dulles, outside of DC. Bigger planes originated from there, ones with larger storage compartments underneath, for our 80-pound furbaby. The morning he loaded her up and drove away to DC was the last I ever saw of either of them. My husband and my furry daughter, gone from my life forever.

They arrived in Bocas and Calle settled into island life.

From: Fabio
To: Erin
Subject: Almost Perfect Day
Date: May 23, 2018 at 6:16:20 PM EDT

If only you were here.
I so want to regain your trust and not have you fear being with me.
Even though I am happier and feel better being here nothing feels quite right without you.
This was supposed to be our place.
Our little shanty town.
I miss you.
I am a flawed person. I have let my fears control me for too long and as a result I have hurt the people I love the most.
I can and want to change many of these things except one – my love for you.
I know you need to see a lot more to believe in me and us.
These words keep echoing in my head and will forever be how I feel about you…
Love is Love, is Love, is Love, is Love, is Love…

From: Fabio
To: Erin
Subject: Re: Love is Love
Date: July 19, 2018 at 7:56:33 PM EDT

My final word of the day
I have never wanted anything more than to be Your Man.
I hope I get there but I know if I don't – I will die still trying.

I wanted to believe everything he wrote but behind closed doors is where the real truth lies. I rejected all his hoovering attempts and doubled down in the condo alone. "Get your happy on Fabio, then call for me. I've been trying to make you happy for 20 years; it's your turn now."

Once I'd signed off on the agreement his mood seemed to lighten. I told myself that having it made him feel more secure and that the fresh air and a six-month break would help him calm down and reflect on our marriage. Nothing could be farther from the truth. In fact, he was setting up his master plan to divorce me while lining up his next source of supply. So cool, so calculated, and with razor-sharp precision, he carefully unraveled everything we'd built together one step at a time.

After he signed the agreement, with our realtor Randy acting as his witness, and without advance notice to me, all credit cards were canceled and joint bank accounts closed, with the remaining funds transferred to Panama. Suddenly, my phone no longer had a data plan. I called the phone company and learned that he'd lowered it down to 1GB so I couldn't navigate or go anywhere. My EZPass no longer worked and when I went to Costco they made me sign up for a new account, explaining that he'd called to have my name removed. I phoned him to ask why he was doing all of this and he flatly denied everything, calling me delusional and paranoid. He's a smart cookie; he learned everything from his dad, the attorney, to never write down anything threatening, but the phone calls I had with him during this time were absolutely terrifying. I wished I'd taped him.

Before he shut everything down, I saw on our joint credit card that he had retained an attorney so I asked him about it.

"Oh, that? Well, that was just in case you were going to divorce me," he lied.

"Well, I'm not," I responded.

The denial of what was really happening had taken over my ability to see clearly. Covert narcissists rarely initiate divorce but they will make your life a living hell until you divorce them. That way, they can remain the victim and procure sympathy from their new source of supply. *Oh, poor me, she was craazy, she cheated on me and left me.* But I was stronger than he bargained for, but sadly, to my own detriment.

The truth is, I WAS afraid of him. The times I'd seen him dissociate, the secrets, the lies, the running away rather than working things out. "I am afraid to come to Bocas ever since you left me in Lancaster and the multiple times you've run out the door when things don't go your way. I can't trust you. I can't depend on you. I cannot give up my entire life for someone I cannot trust, who does not trust me, and I cannot depend on to be there if things go wrong. Would you? Who would, Fabio?"

I just wanted him to stop being mean to me, to change because he loved me, but people don't change, everyone knows that. Everyone except Erin, who thinks her love is so strong she can fix just about anything.

"Big question… if you don't show your true self, who was I supposed to fall in love with? The fake persona you concocted to keep from being close to other humans, thereby avoiding any pain?" Backfire.

He emailed me the words I wished were true:

"I still have faith in us."

"I am not trying to rush us toward a divorce."

"Even so, I still don't want a divorce so I'm not doing anything about that either."

"You asked me the other day if I was afraid to have sex with someone else/new. Another difference between us is that I am not really thinking about that prospect. I have been way more focused on if I'm ever going to get to be back with you again."

From: Fabio
To: Erin
Subject: LOML
Date: November 21, 2018 at 8:56:15 AM EST

"As I said many times before Erin, you are the love of my life."

Two weeks later, it came, by email no less, without advance warning or discussion – the final discard.

From: Fabio
To: Erin
Subject: LOML
Date: December 6, 2018 at 8:20:52 PM EST

Reluctantly, I had my attorney file for Divorce with the Montgomery County court and you will get an official notification from her in the next day or two via Certified Mail.

"Why?" I asked him.

From: Fabio
To: Erin
Subject: Why?
Date: December 9, 2018 at 5:21:21 PM EST

I do not want this to be adversarial. I will try to answer your 'why' question below. I'm feeling more confusion than anything else. I am surprised by your reaction.

Why did I file? You mean aside from being told by you for most of the past year and a half or more that you are afraid of me?

Here are some quotes from emails you have written in just the past two weeks:

"I want a man who loves and respects me and I'm going to find him."

"Please find a woman who wants what you have to give. You have many talents and skills but this theory of yours that opposites attract is not sustainable for me. I was very unhappy for a very long time and felt shut out and dismissed."

"Please find someone who goes with your thing because it just brings me down."

Did you really think you could take a six-month break, without breaking us? *Yes, Fabio, I did.*

This all sounds like it is coming from someone who wants a divorce. You have been talking to me like this for over a year and a half so I don't think my filing should either be a surprise or seem like I am rushing anything.

All that said - it all still feels strange without you. I never wanted any of this. I feel like I tried to save us a hundred times. As much as I still love you (even though you say I don't) I can't go on anymore under this cloud of anger and resentment from you. You clearly don't want to be with me - what else am I supposed to do?

I don't know, change? Be nice, honest, vulnerable? I guess not. It was just too much to ask.

My heart sank. I wanted to be married forever, to stroll the streets of our shanty town and walk hand in hand on our beach together. I only wanted to make him happy and for him to trust me. But he never was and he never could. Those girls at the pool did us in long before we met.

He'd already unfriended and blocked my son and me and deleted every picture of our lives together from his social media. It's like we never happened. Just like the wedding suit he left hanging in the closet, Birkenstocks below, when he abandoned me in Lancaster and emptied out the condo.

He never even said goodbye to Julian, his stepson of 20 years.

"It's like we've been completely erased and replaced," Julian said. "He didn't just steal everything you ever owned Mom, he stole your entire life."

Gratefully, he didn't get my soul. My soul is mine to keep and my soul is a survivor.

Looking at the relationship from an outside perspective, Julian was able to see things more clearly than I could. After 20 years of psychological and emotional abuse, my brain was like mashed potatoes.

"You know how he got away with it don't you, Mom? Everything he ever said was delivered in the same deadpan, sarcastic way. We couldn't tell if he was kidding or serious, but we wanted to believe he was just kidding." Otherwise, the pain of the truth, that he hated us that much, was a cross too big for us to bear.

Like Dar, Julian is a sage.

In January 2019, a month after he filed for divorce, I contacted our Panamanian attorney to discuss transferring the property to Fabio and she asked me, "Were you aware that Fabio gave himself a majority interest in the Panama property?"

"No," came my stunned reply.

"I knew it," she said. "I should have contacted you. I thought maybe you knew, or that the two of you had some kind of arrangement, but it just didn't seem right to me as a married couple."

She'd never seen anyone do that to someone before and she's a lawyer! He had written the legal papers in Spanish knowing I didn't speak the language and would never find out. He made himself President and Secretary of the Panamanian corporation that owned the Bocas property and as Secretary, awarded himself full signing privileges, which is how he assigned himself the majority interest in the stock certificates. He held on to them for years before finally handing them over for her to file with the Panamanian government when we took our final vacation there in February 2018. He picked at his hands frantically during the entire 30-minute cab ride from the airport to the immigration office. I knew something was seriously amiss but had no idea that he was sitting right next to me, stealing the house from me, right under my nose.

A section of the "Temporary" Separation agreement we'd signed the previous summer required us to file our 2018 tax return as a married couple; it was the last legal hurdle before the divorce would be finalized. It was my responsibility to hire a business accountant to complete the final tax return for Rock & Roll After School and as he had every year since we were married, Fabio would take care of doing our personal return. The K1, which showed proceeds from the sale of the business, was due on March 31st, but the accountant I'd hired did not deliver it that day.

My phone rang. It was Fabio, or shall I say, the monster that lurked deep within my "loving" husband. I could feel his rage through the phone. "Where's my K1?" he growled, in a most intimidating fashion, to which I calmly offered, "Let me call the accountant and I'll get back to you, okay?" The next thing I knew, he was threatening to report me and the business accountant to the IRS before even giving me the chance to follow up with him. Once I did, I found out he'd filed for an extension, perfectly legal and above board, giving him another week to finish up. Fabio didn't care. When Fabio says "do it," you'd better do it.

I tried one final time, in May of 2019, to try and stop him from throwing away everything we'd worked for together over the past 20 years. "Please," I begged him, "slow down. We don't need to divorce; we could just be separated for a bit longer until we both calm down from all that's happened in the past year." It was the last chance I had to save what I had worked my entire life for and that's when he let the scariest monster yet, come out.

"I'm going to destroy you, Erin," he screamed at me through the phone. "You know I can, and I WILL do it!"

From December 2018 when he filed to the following June, I represented myself "Pro Se," which in Latin means "in one's own behalf." I'd learned so much about how the court system works from all the times Fabio played me like a puppet during the child support and custody lawsuits with my first husband, and the more recent ones with our landlords. I knew I didn't need to waste money on an attorney just to lose everything; I could file all the necessary legal papers by myself.

I filed what's known as an emergency QDRO, a Qualified Domestic Relations Order, to protect whatever was left of the pension from his corporate pharmaceutical job. In the end, I received only 30% of our financial assets, and when I look back on it and think about who he truly is, I feel lucky to have received anything at all. I was even more fortunate to have the condo in King of Prussia so I'd have a safe place to live, and the value on that property just keeps going up. I guess he knew I was smart enough and had just enough strength left to make sure I could at least live indoors, even if it wouldn't be overlooking the Caribbean. I was grateful to be alive and given the chance to rebuild my life.

The day before I had to go to court and stand before the Judge, I contacted the very same Domestic Violence organization in Chester County that had provided me with no-cost counseling back in 2017. They offered me top-notch counsel on a single day's notice to accompany me to divorce court in Montgomery County. She stayed up half the night to research my case and showed up like a shark on my behalf. Reach out, there are organizations that can help you.

Fabio did not appear in court to divorce me and the Judge took note of it saying, "He's a coward and he knows it," for not showing up to divorce his wife of 15 years. Fabio listened in on the phone from Panama while both lawyers gasped in disbelief. After the hearing was over, the Judge pulled me aside and told me to reach out to him if there was any problem enforcing the QDRO. "Snakes like him don't deserve girls like you."

Yes I am a silly girl, for not having seen sooner that you were nothing but a coward with a heart full of fear.

We would never go diving around the world or sail the Caribbean islands together. He would never take me to the Paris dive where they sing and dance on the bar all night like he promised. It was all a lie, and it had been since the very first day he met me and decided I looked like an easy target.

Our divorce was finalized on July 15, 2019; Julian's 27th birthday was two days later. In the 20 years we'd been together, Fabio's mom had been his "grandma;" he called her GiGi Evelyn, just like all the other grandkids did. Since Stephen's mom passed long before Julian was born, Evelyn was the only grandmother he knew besides my mom, and he loved her. He waited a week, then two weeks, and for the first time since he was seven years old, no birthday card arrived. He was deeply hurt. His stepfather stole his inheritance and left the country without saying goodbye, and now his grandmother had forgotten his birthday.

I emailed her. I had to stick up for my son. He was an innocent bystander yet he was hurt more than anyone. "Evelyn, could you please keep being his GiGi?" I pleaded. "You don't need to speak to me if you don't want to but he's devastated." She did reply, but only to ask for his address so she could respond to him directly.

Julian received proof of Evelyn's cold cruelty in the form of a hand-written letter saying she didn't believe me when I wrote that he was devastated, and then justified why she didn't send him a birthday card. She was too busy, she's old, she'd had a car accident the year before, and if he wanted to stay in touch HE could write to her. If he did, she promised to respond. Dismissed forever in an instant by his grandmother, stepdad, and every one of his uncles and his aunt. My sweet son Julian, who didn't do a single thing to deserve any of it.

"If you're not at lunch, you ARE lunch."

I was incensed and wrote to her again. "Think about it Evelyn, why would I spend seven years designing and building my dream retirement home, put $145,000 of my own hard-earned money into it, become a permanent Panamanian resident, and ship every single one of my belongings yet never move there or even get to see the house again? It doesn't add up, does it? Your son pulled a fast one. If there is anything here that you do not believe, just tell me. I have written proof of everything, including the gaslighting story about my $100,000 prenup he stole and his multiple threats, but something tells me, deep down, you know I'm telling the truth."

She'd tried to warn me about him, in her own covert way, on her very first visit to our home in Valley Forge when she said, "Have you ever noticed how negative he is? He's always been a loner; he's never had any friends." She never responded and my son and I never heard from her again.

32.
BECOMING FRIENDS WITH LAURA (FIRST WIFE): FEBRUARY 2019

The psychologist who administered our testing suggested I reach out to Fabio's first wife to ask if her experience with him was in any way similar to mine. I found her contact info online and dialed the number. She seemed surprised to hear from me but happy nonetheless and we agreed to meet. Laura had always tried to be friendly to me but Fabio would call her crazy and unhinged and pointed out several reasons over the years to support that narrative. By now it was clear to me who was actually crazy and it wasn't her. We scheduled a lunch together in Red Bank, NJ, at a pretty restaurant overlooking the water, close to where she lived.

That lunch lasted four-and-a-half hours. The waiters were circling about, cleaning up, and getting ready to close between lunch and dinner, so we asked if we could stay just a bit longer. No problem; they could tell it was important and we were allowed to finish our conversation. That day was incredibly healing for both of us. When you are abused in secret you crave validation for all of the suffering you've endured. The most difficult thing about surviving life with a master manipulator is to be gaslit all over again by those who say, "Well, there are two sides to every story," or "It couldn't have been that bad; he's so quiet, and seems like such a great guy."

With tears in her eyes, she told me she believed him, that she was the one who was crazy. He and I stayed together for 20 years and from the outside, it appeared to be a happy marriage. No, Laura, you're not crazy, not at all. Everything you are telling me is a mirror image of the life I suffered with him, from the robotic, canned phrases and sexual dysfunction to the black-eyed, raging monster she and I both feared might hurt us physically.

I told her everything. She looked back at me, wide-eyed, and thanked me for reaching out. She had suffered alone for nearly 30 years. He'd intentionally poisoned their only daughter against her, a wound much deeper than I believed I may suffer one day by his hand. He made fun of her when she'd had a miscarriage, called her crazy right to her face, and worse yet, behind her back to their daughter. "Layla, you know you have to find a way to get along with your mom, even though she's *craazy*." He'd stonewalled her and blamed her for all the troubles in their marriage. Sounds familiar, right?

Her very first question to me was a disturbing one, but the first one any concerned and loving mother would need the answer to.

"I have to know; did he sexually abuse her?"

I took a deep breath and told her, "Maybe; I think so, but probably not in the way you are most worried about."

I proceeded to tell her about all the nights when he would lock her bedroom door for "Daddy-Daughter Alone Time." "But Laura, he told me that was your request. That you didn't want Layla to feel threatened by me, that she was losing her dad. 'Daddy-Daughter Alone Time' is what you and Layla called it; that's what he always said."

Her eyes told me the truth. My heart broke in two, for Laura but even more for Layla.

"Layla's friends are all getting married now and having kids, but she doesn't think it will ever happen for her," Laura shared.

I thought back to all the times I told him that, and all the times he rolled his eyes at me and dismissed my concern.

"I thought he hated my personality," she sighed.

"Bingo." I always thought I annoyed him by just being me and trying to make him happy. I was the ballerina in the jewelry box who would pop up and twirl but he would quickly shut the lid and the music would stop, leaving me crumpled over and broken, only to pop up and try all over again.

The next day, I received a text that I hold on to and read in times of self-doubt.

"I felt so understood. Like you are the only person who knows what I went through." I responded with a resounding, "I AM!"

He made fun of anyone who appeared happy or blindly trusting, or even the slightest bit positive. We were all fools. The world is a dangerous place to Fabio and he knows that intimately because he is the one who is inherently dangerous.

Laura and I are forever sisters. There's no way two completely different women can survive a narcissistic marriage to the same man and not come out as besties. She treated me to a Broadway show to celebrate my newfound freedom, we support each other by phone, and we chuckle together about what we both survived. "Fabio, whatcha doing?" BIG PAUSE.

"Nothing," giving me her best Eeyore impression.

"No Laura, you responded far too quickly, longer pause next time!" We giggle. If we couldn't laugh together we'd cry, so we laugh.

I'm grateful that he and I never had any children of our own. We talked about it when we first moved in together but he said he wanted our relationship to improve first. In truth, he didn't want his daughter to be jealous of a new baby and manipulated the situation to his benefit.

A new baby would permanently cement our partnership and would make it more difficult for him to triangulate his daughter and me against each other.

Looking back, I was luckier than Laura. Poisoning a child against their other parent is a crime deserving of the worst possible punishment. There's a special place in hell for people who do that. He tried to sway my friends and family against me too but was never successful; they just didn't like him all that much. We'd spent our 20 years together on my turf and I was smart to have retained most of my relationships throughout that period.

Next stop… repairing things with Layla. I started with an email. "I'm sad that your dad made such an issue out of this, and so freaking weird that rather than just introduce us after we'd been dating a few weeks or months, he was trying to devise some roundabout, backward way of 'running into each other' at the grocery store and offering to feed my cats. Completely awkward and unnecessary; it just made things worse from the get-go." She totally agreed. If we had been allowed to develop our relationship organically and without his need to triangulate, we could have been the best of friends. She's a remarkable young woman and I miss her humor and her smarts.

33.

NEXT VICTIM, PLEASE

Idealize, Devalue, Discard, Hoover, Idealize, Devalue, Discard, Hoover… the cycle of abuse continues.

In January 2019, one month after he filed for divorce, a friend from Bocas called to tell me he was seen walking down Blave Beach Road with a blond woman who turned out to be the person he was referring to when he said he was so impressed with his brother Milo who "always had one waiting in the wings." I'll never know for sure but I would imagine he'd been talking with her online for quite some time now and flew her to Bocas to meet in person. Remember, I chose him because I thought he would NEVER cheat. He was so uncomfortable with women, so shy and awkward. But as my friend Holly says, "You've got to watch out for the quiet ones; they're up to no good."

So like any curious gal, I looked her up online and could see he may have moved a bit hastily. He wasn't going to allow himself to be cheated on again and swiftly identified his next target. Low-hanging fruit from what I can tell. She's lived a transient life over the past few years. A pretty girl but looks much older than her actual age, and the clincher… she's a psychic, and a hairdresser. *Lol, you had me at psychic!* I know him like the back of my hand and I'll bet he thinks she's beneath him and would be easy prey once she's been captured. I imagined all the dismissive jokes trapped inside of his head, but a narcissist does not exist without supply and cannot be choosy when living on a remote Panamanian island desperately looking for someone – anyone – to move there with him.

I found Karma's psychic page on Facebook and chuckled to myself. She's a self-proclaimed "empath,"[62] believes in the paranormal, and claims she can bring back the dead. I can feel him cringing now. His name for Laura was the "Esthetician-Dog Walker," an insult meaning he considered her beneath him. Karma must be the "Psychic-Hairdresser," so he can feel superior to her too. She eventually stopped posting on her psychic page just after saying she was going to be more active. I'm sure there were passive-aggressive remarks made by him about it; it's stupid or simply rolled his eyes at her, something to that effect. I wonder what my name is now, besides Crazy. Perhaps Needy-Crazy? Needy-Crazy-Talks to herself? Yeah, probably that, but probably even worse.

I anonymously mailed his psych report to her twin sister

------

[62] "Empath" • Someone highly attuned to the feelings and emotions of others, sometimes actually taking those feelings on themselves at a deep emotional level. (Though professionals disagree on whether such people exist.)

in Maine but she still stayed with him in Panama. I can only imagine what lies he's told her about it… I'd made it all up, I'M the one who's crazy, I MADE him crazy or, you should see HER report! I'm guessing Karma is also experiencing a degree of cognitive dissonance because otherwise she might be homeless. Part of me feels sorry for her but I tried to warn her. Maybe one day she'll believe me and not waste as many years with him as I did.

I wish Laura had warned me. I wouldn't have believed her at the time but at some point, I would have had to. Laura wishes she'd never even met him. They share a daughter and that's just the saddest thing of all. I've done my civic duty here; the rest belongs to the Universe. I likely bought her a few extra years of love bombing by sending it. He will need to hold back his negative behaviors to prove to her that I am the one who is crazy.

In February 2020, just before the beginning of the COVID-19 pandemic, I received an email from him telling me he'd put our dog Calle down. My daughter of more than 10 years and I never even got to say goodbye to her. He made all the decisions; I never had a say in anything. When I first met him I mistook this for his taking care of me, but in the end, it was my biggest downfall to allow him to get away with it for so long. My replacement, Karma, was with her as the veterinarian put her to sleep forever. I cried like I've never cried before. *How could I have spent 20 years with someone who could be so cruel?*

I emailed him one final time, to tell him I knew about Karma. "I bet you wish you could undo everything you did, if not for anything else but the money." What he did and the way he did it only added to his negative self-narrative, that he is a bad person and deserves to be banished.

I continued, "You'll never have that boat you wanted, and hey if Karma is a psychic, how come she didn't warn us about the pandemic?" Ha, ha… Guess what happened next? He bought a boat, probably by liquidating half his share of the pension. You know what they call a boat, don't you? A boat is a hole in the water you throw money into. I now see him for who he really is – a scared little boy.

The last thing I saw online of the two of them together confirmed to me that nothing about him has changed, and while it is early in their relationship, he is still filled with secrets that can hurt, and it will all come out eventually.

I stumbled across a video of them on Facebook receiving their new boat in Bocas del Toro. The video begins with the boat being delivered to them at the dock and then it cuts to the two of them together on the boat. Karma is videotaping and is heard saying, "It's our maiden voyage!" No response at all from Fabio, absolutely nothing… no glance her way, no smile of acknowledgment, not one single word given to connect with her excitement for their new boat. Later in the video she says, "LOVING the water," and then, somewhat garbled, "Isn't it great to be out on the water?" and again, he says absolutely nothing.

Trying to connect a third time, she moves around to the front of the boat pointing the camera directly at his face but he won't even look her way; no acknowledgment of any kind. I remembered exactly what this felt like. It felt like complete emptiness, my heart would sink to the ground, but then my logical brain would kick in and create the cognitive dissonance to explain it away so that I wouldn't have to leave him or hurt him.

I imagined her saying to herself, "He probably didn't hear me because of the wind," or "I shouldn't have interrupted him, he's learning the controls for our new boat." It's a tactic narcissists use to keep you small, to keep you walking on eggshells. It's called stonewalling[63] and it's always intentional no matter what they tell you. *I'm thinking! I want to give you a thoughtful response. I process information more slowly than you.* Bullshit, each and every time. They are concocting the response that will best serve them.

I felt the same vacant hole I'd come to know so intimately whenever he would do this to me. It was like I was looking directly through her eyes, only to witness the same cold, stern person my husband had become – my abuser. I'd rather be alone than be lonely with someone else.

That was all the concrete evidence I needed to see to know for sure that he is up to his old tricks and the cycle only repeats itself. As long as I remember how I *felt* in those moments and not what I *think* about them, I'll be fine. His one-word answers, the aloofness; I don't miss it. Thank goodness, I can finally feel my feelings again. I

---

[63] "Stonewalling" • The term for when a person decides to deliberately stop communicating or cooperating to frustrate or punish the other party.

can cry now and it feels beautiful. I can even write a book about it.

The last thing to do, to close the door on this chapter of my life, was to attempt to get my premarital possessions back, but the cost to return them was astronomical and it was rare that a shipping container was ever headed back to the States. Fabio only offered to leave them in a warehouse by the airport a few miles away and it would be my responsibility to get everything the remaining 4,000 miles back to Pennsylvania.

In May of 2020, three months into the COVID-19 pandemic, I decided to email Karma directly to ask for help getting my things back. I knew Fabio would keep whatever he could just to be mean. I didn't even know if she knew he was married when she first began dating him and planning her move from Maine into the retirement home he and I had built together. We'd named our Panamanian corporation, "Truwuv Propiedades," an homage to the movie that first brought us together, *The Princess Bride*. It was the theme of our wedding and a phrase he repeated to me hundreds of times whenever I asked him to do something for me, only this time, in Spanish.

I wasn't surprised to receive no response from her so I only got back whatever he was willing to give me and the rest of my personal property still decorates their house. She may not realize it yet but she is the next frog in the pot of boiling water and the water only gets hotter. Personally, I'd be completely creeped out if I were her, with memories of our 20 years together everywhere you turn. Bad juju, Karma. Very bad juju.

A girlfriend in Panama helped me hire a couple of local workers with a truck to collect whatever I was "allowed" to have back. I hired a young pregnant woman and her husband to stage a yard sale and they sold everything to raise money to feed the indigenous families during the pandemic. Bocas del Toro's economy is 100% reliant on tourism and the Panamanian government only offered an $80-per-month "Bono"[64] for a family of four. I may have lost every possession I ever owned but we raised over $5,000 to feed hungry families. Being a good codependent it felt good to help others, even if from a distance, and in line with the intention I'd set for myself by moving there in the first place. *Stuff is just stuff, I reassured myself. Your life is worth so much more.*

Karma posted a tour of the house on YouTube displaying many of the premarital personal possessions he'd refused to return. The handmade glass bug tiles from our Valley Forge kitchen that my friend Roger and I designed and created together. The blue and yellow candle votives from the GRAMMY event I produced featuring The Fugees; my flower-shaped tealight holders lined up along the deck railing. The Kitchen-Aid mixer I used to bake cookies with my friend Joy for over 30 years, and the blue ceramic bowl I made Julian's Sunday pancakes in when he was just a boy, all gone.

---

[64] "Bono" • The Panamanian version of "Unemployment Insurance."

I'd purchased a glass ball floor lamp from Restoration Hardware to match the table lamp he gave me for my 42nd birthday; now Karma and I have matching lamps, and the tropical bedroom lamp with painted metal palm leaves that my dad bought me from the Bombay Company at the mall. But the most heartbreaking thing to see was the blue glass iced-tea pitcher on the kitchen counter given to me by my now deceased friend Nancy Falkow, who sang us a love song at our wedding at Holly Hedge. They are surrounded by his past failures; ghosts of me are everywhere. They are only material possessions, but the sea glass collection I started on Cape Cod and added to from every beach I'd ever visited in my lifetime was priceless to me and he knew it. He is the Punisher and from his perspective, I deserved to lose everything.

I wouldn't want to be completely isolated with him. When we lived together he was on my turf. I had friends and family all around me. I know what happens over time; it happened to his first fiancé, his first wife, and then to me. I'm grateful to be out of his narcissistic clutches and be able to move on with my life. My health has greatly improved and my attitude and happiness have skyrocketed.

34.
PROCESSING, ACCEPTANCE, AND RECOVERY

I discovered tons of free resources on YouTube – educational videos about narcissism and codependency – and used my pandemic time to learn everything I could about them. My two favorites are Dr. Ramani, a clinical psychologist, known for her expertise on narcissistic personality disorder and narcissistic abuse, and Lisa A. Romano, a savvy and sassy girl from Queens, who survived a similar experience married to her first husband for 13 years. These two ladies saved my sanity.

Dr. Ramani suggests writing an "Ick List," journaling every memory about the narcissist that made you feel icky so you remember how you *felt* and not what you *thought,* and so you don't glorify them in the aftermath. The false self they present is *almost* ironclad. My list is several pages long.

Lisa A. Romano's stories made me laugh when all I wanted to do was cry. Her personal experience and expertise on the subject were so helpful for me to understand what had happened. She likens it to a chicken caught up in a tornado. While you're in the relationship you're spinning around not knowing up from down, just trying to stay alive until eventually, you are violently flung a mile or so away, look back and say to yourself, "Damn, that was a REALLY BIG TORNADO." Ha, ha, Lisa. Thanks.

There are many great analogies to illustrate what it feels like to be caught in the grips of one of these abusers and why you often don't realize what is happening to you until it's too late. The proverbial frog in boiling water, a spider spinning its web, a cat toying with and terrorizing a mouse before eating it alive.

I can't blame Fabio for everything; I am a 50% contributor by allowing it. I've since learned everything there is to know about narcissism and codependency and the toxic dance these two personality types bring to a relationship. The narcissist is self-focused and the codependent is other-focused. What a perfect pairing (NOT)! I have a black belt in narcissism now; I could teach a college course in it. No narc will ever fool me again.

If he had ever hit me I'd have known to leave, but he never did. After he was gone I began experiencing severe PTSD[65] symptoms. Nightmares of him grabbing a kitchen knife during an argument and stabbing me in the heart in a dissociative rage. I could see his angry, black eyes hovering over me as I fell limply to the ground. The next thing I knew I was out of my body, watching

---

[65] "PTSD" • Post-Traumatic Stress Disorder

him from above, realizing what he'd just done, and then cutting me up into a hundred pieces to bury me deep in the jungle. I wasn't going to let that happen to me.

I'm sure if you spoke to him he would claim I was the abuser. It conveniently fits his narrative that HE is the victim, but the signs are clear; my angry responses were a result of years of abuse, and what's known as reactive abuse.[66]

Abusers rely on this; it gives them "proof" the victim is irrational or mentally ill, and they hold these reactions against you indefinitely when it's simply self-defense in the face of an onslaught of punishment. True victims feel bad about their behavior because it isn't normal for them; they possess empathy and express remorse.

Trauma lives on in the body – read *The Body Keeps the Score*.[67] In the end my well-honed, fight/flight survival brain is what saved me. I'd been practicing yoga for over 20 years; it kept me flexible, resilient, and strong. Meditation and mindfulness training prevented me from ruminating about what happened, circling back over it again and again in my mind. Listening to Taylor Swift songs on repeat while dancing around my apartment in my undies kept me smiling too. She sure has some good breakup songs!

---

[66] "Reactive Abuse" • When a victim retaliates after gaslighting, manipulation, and other types of controlling behavior.

[67] van der Kolk, B. A. (2014). *The Body Keeps the Score: Brain, mind, and body in the healing of trauma.* Viking.

In June of 2020, I got a French Bulldog puppy and called him Murphy, for the little girl who felt invisible and unloved. It was the nickname my dad had given me as a baby before I became Birdie. He's been the best companion, proving to me that you CAN buy unconditional love!

Best of all, I finally figured out how to use the TV remotes. It took me a year from the day he left, but I did it!

Nervous to meet someone new, I tippy-toed into online dating and met a very special man who would give me hope for the future. We were both just out of relationships so the timing wasn't exactly right but he was the first thing I could actually feel in over 20 years. I memorialized that meeting with a commissioned art piece drawn by my friend Jamie, which hangs on the wall in my living room to remind me to wait for the "lightning bolt" and not rationalize my feelings ever again or convince myself I can fix things. A healthy relationship with a real man would be possible once I'd peeled away all the layers and done the work I needed to do. I keep his spirit in my heart to remind me of what love *feels* like. Meeting him proved to me that magic exists in the world, and maybe, just maybe, some of it is meant for me.

I was invited to be a guest on *The Behavioral Corner*[68] podcast and received support and validation from others who had survived similar circumstances. This book is for

---

[68] "The Behavioral Corner" • A podcast and multimedia concern dealing primarily with behavioral health.

them, and for anyone questioning whether or not they are in a toxic relationship.

Toward the very end of the interview, host Steve Martorano spoke the words that showed me he truly understood what I'd been through.

"Who WAS that guy? And what level was he operating on?"

The key word here is Operating. My friend George also understood. "Geez, Erin, that's the kind of shit Tyler and I see on *Dateline!*"

In the end, Fabio did me a favor. I'm grateful he was the one who discarded me because I would never have left him, would never have divorced him. *I am not a quitter!* I never once cheated on him or lied to him, I never stole a thing, and I never would. I never even once spoke out of turn about him to any of my friends and would have died of loneliness in that marriage just trying to make him happy.

Neither of my husbands loved me. I was "selected" by each of them, based on specific criteria. Stephen needed someone to help him take care of his three kids; that's why he introduced me to them so quickly. I passed that test with flying colors. He needed a permanent place to live and I'd just purchased my first home, and bonus – he could get backstage to meet rock stars and play his guitar with them.

Fabio knew I owned my Manayunk home outright and had zero debt. He had a rented condo and a lot of debt. I also had a prestigious career and a ton of friends. If he could capture me he would get it all by proxy. I fell for their love bombing hook, line, and sinker. I wanted to feel seen, to be heard – just like Tommy Walker – something I'd never felt as a child left alone to raise herself.

Every interaction with a narcissist is transactional and intentional but there is a major difference between my first and second husbands. Stephen is absolutely brilliant and determined to come out on top in every situation. He uses all the standard narcissistic tricks – love bombing, triangulation, and blame-shifting. He makes lightning-quick decisions in order to remain number one in real-time. He can lie, cheat, or steal from anyone, even his own kids.

But with Fabio it was also premeditated, diabolical, and carefully calculated. He planned retaliation on anyone who disrespected him; the slightest infraction was considered a cross worthy of punishment. He was sneaky about it too, so as not to be discovered. *He who has nothing to hide, hides nothing.* This is how he protected himself from being hurt, by hurting those around him first.

35.

IN CLOSING

Not all narcissists are grandiose; some operate under the radar. They call these narcissists covert or vulnerable and they are far more dangerous and difficult to spot. They are reserved and aloof, but deeply insecure.

Abusers abuse in secret. They carefully vet and select a single target to then project their internal misery onto it. They make a quick real-time assessment of a person or situation and spring into action. No one outside the home will know the pain you are suffering, and many will not believe you. You may be gaslit again and again by unknowing people who tell you... it couldn't have been that bad, there are two sides to every story, and you have to admit, you are kind of a bitch sometimes, right? You may even gaslight yourself and wonder if the problem really was you all along, and perhaps if you'd done something differently or handled it a different way, you might have changed the outcome. I can assure you that narcissists are not capable of changing. They do not see you, cannot hear you, and do not even want to. They don't love you; they don't even like you.

Some of the final thoughts I shared with him:

"Like I said Fabio, hatred. You miss the target of your rage and that's me. Am I your mom that you resent for putting you in charge of your sibs?"

"Love is not cruel, dismissive, or secretive but all I got was the secretive, defensive, denying, dismissive shape-shifter who screams at me."

Being married to a covert narcissist is comparable to being brainwashed by a cult or kidnapped and held captive, developing a version of Stockholm syndrome called a trauma bond.[69] A victim may not even be aware they're being abused because cognitive dissonance alters their perceived reality. The abuse is masked intentionally and completely invisible to those outside the marriage, and often to the victim themselves.

Take notice to observe how you *feel* around someone and not what you *think* based on what they say. Wait for that magic, those butterflies, and don't rationalize when it comes to matters of the heart. Trust your gut. Your gut is there to tell you what's right for you. It knows you better than you do and it's trying to protect you.

It takes a lot of time to undo years of narcissistic abuse but I promise you will make it through. You will rise

---

[69] "Trauma Bond" • Occurs when the abused person forms an unhealthy bond with the person who abuses them. The abused may develop sympathy for the abuser slowly reinforced by repeated cycles of abuse followed by remorse.

like a Phoenix and no one will ever be able to abuse you again.

When looking back over the 20 years we spent together, I came to the realization that he gave himself credit for the successes we shared and any problems we faced were all due to me. No one should have to live like that; that is not a marriage. Marriage is an equal partnership, a bond of love and shared respect that creates a powerful love energy that feeds the entire universe with positivity.

Give yourself time, however long it takes to heal. Learn who you are and what makes you truly happy. Take a good look inside your soul to learn how you arrived at this point in your life and what you can do going forward to become the best version of yourself possible. Take the reins of your own life and gift yourself true happiness and self-love. Knowing your true self will keep you safe from predators.

Self-forgiveness is the final and most necessary part of the journey out of a toxic relationship. You do not know what you do not know and you must forgive yourself for trying to help the wrong person. Only then can you begin to heal the generational trauma of your ancestors. It's a gift of healing that is paid forward to your children, their children, and to the world.

Psychological damage can happen as a result of early trauma; it happened to both of us and the dance we did together was a toxic one. I tried so hard to love him, I gave it everything I had but I just couldn't *feel* him. I tried to save him from his misery but never felt connected to him while he was lying to me, accusing me of all the things he was doing, and keeping secrets. I kept on wishing, kept on trying. I desperately wanted to fix him so he could be my lover and best friend for life, but happiness comes from within, not from others. You cannot make an unhappy person happy. All you can do is make yourself happy and let the unhappy people do the same, if they even can. You've always had the power, my dear, you just had to learn it for yourself.[70]

A few months after he left for Panama I traveled to Houston and completed a 21-day lemon water fast. It was akin to an exorcism. With all the stress I'd been living with for the past two decades I was afraid of developing an autoimmune disease and wanted to give my body a healthy, fresh start. Once that fast was completed there was one final step to close this chapter of my life once and for all. I'd read about the magical healing powers of the sacred teacher plant ayahuasca[71] and set off on a pilgrimage to learn all I could from "her." I participated in three life-changing ceremonies that connected me back to my inner child and higher self.

---

[70] "The Wizard of Oz" • Paraphr. Vidor, King, Victor Fleming, George Cukor, Richard Thorpe, Norman Taurog, and Mervyn LeRoy. 1939. *The Wizard of Oz*. United States: Metro-Goldwyn-Mayer (MGM).

[71] "Ayahuasca" • A brew made from the Banisteriopsis caapi and Psychotria viridis plants, native to the Amazon region, noted for its hallucinogenic properties.

Before sitting with The Mother, as they so lovingly call her, I was only able to express two emotions – happy or angry. Sad? What's sad? You are not allowed to be sad, Erin; you look ugly when you do that. I cried in Ceremony, for the little girl who deserved more love, and am forever changed through self-love. I can feel her spiritual teachings; they now reside deep within my soul. Once I returned home I burned white sage sticks and danced around my home like a tiny ballerina but this time no one closed the lid on me and I knew in my heart that no one ever could again.

He is where he belongs now, living on a remote island, tucked away from people – people who can't hurt him any longer and whom he can no longer hurt.

If anything happens to me, you all know who did it.

THE END

47989CB00009B/3059